Breakthrough Copywriter

A Field Guide to the Advertising Genius of Eugene M. Schwartz

Edited by **Dr. Robert C. Worstell**

Copyright © 2014, 2016 Midwest Journal Press.
All Rights Reserved

Table of Contents

Forward..1
   Notes on Usage:..3
   How to Study This Book.......................................4
Introduction..6
What the *Copywriter* Needs to Know......................9
   A. Copywriting Basics..9
   B. How to align mass desire onto your product.................11
   C. What Your Prospect's State of Awareness Demands From Your Headline..................13
   D. Know the Stages of Sophistication of your Market..........16
   E. The 7 Basic Techniques of Breakthrough Advertising.......17
   F. Additional copywriting skills: Verification - Reinforcement - Interweaving..................28
What Are the "Mass Desires?"..............................31
   6 Key Principles Of Influence By Robert Cialdini..............32
   Maslow's Hierarchy of Needs...................................34
   The Nine Motives..39
   The Four Wants Which Glue Human Experience Together....40
Addendum..42
   Breakthrough Advertising Secrets............................42
Postscript - What This Series Has To Do With You........76
   Preamble..76
   What Story are YOU Living?...................................80
   What's The Difference Between A Good And Bad Copywriter?..................85
   Valuable Copywriters Are Different..........................88
   How A Story "Works"..90
   When Is a (Marketing) Story "Sensible?"...................92
   Versions of AIDA - the Song Sung Forever...............95
   Are You Really Real?..97
   Why These Stories Are Here..................................101
   How to Use this Book to Get Everything You Could Possibly Want..................104
Bonus...106

Forward

The journey you are on (or about to start, if you are really lucky) is one which will take you into realms you perhaps never thought possible.

For we are entering the boundless and limitless land of the Mind. Anything and everything is possible here. You only have to imagine it.

That is the world of "Salesmanship In Print," as John E. Kennedy is credited for defining copywriting. Any material or etheral good can be offered here in exchange for that commodity of money – or even for simple goodwill.

Ad-men are bean-counters and want to know how many sales your copy got for them. Online, they also want to know click-throughs, leads, and conversions.

The real bottom line is that you are helping your potential client to live in a better world, to improve his life to a better one. When you take that viewpoint (or at least argue against it from the devil's advocate) you'll see a new world open up for any product you are offering.

I've done a study of the old classics of copywriting and marketing, only to find that they are really just as valid today in our online and physical sales world as they have ever been. For people haven't changed all that much, just what they consider "interesting."

Out of all the classic books in this study, Eugene Schwartz' "Breakthrough Advertising" was found to be the most basic and most powerful. It's a shame that it's seldom kept in print, and no one has ever done an ebook for it.

This review you are reading is a hopeful solution to that.

I've done what I could within the realm of notes and reviews. This is based on my own study in pursuit of copywriting mastery.

But note that this is only a study, a series of notes to use as a guidebook. It is up to you to follow the footsteps of those who already tested and succeeded in applying the datums they write about.

Through this, there are two additional models which you may want to test every strategy, system, and tactic you read in this book or any of those:

1. **Sales is based on the Golden Rule** – if you want to be successful, you must help others become more successful. That also applies to "making money." The product you write for and sell needs to help your customer improve their own worth. Or you'll never improve your own.

2. **Every customer and client is on their own journey**. They each have a chosen role to play. Your success depends on helping them with that passage – whether you are providing them tools, weapons, or merely advice.

Those are the two principles which have been missing from all classic and modern texts on this subject. By finding these, new dimensions are opened for all marketing, all copywriting.

You'll see as you study Schwartz' work, these tie the loose ends together. You may even see startling new revelations as you start trying to see how these datums fit within. Don't worry – you'll be testing *everything* from here on out. And as you should – no single datum is valuable until it's been tested and proved.

So, let's get going…

Dr. Robert C. Worstell
May 2014

Notes on Usage:

I made my own outline and notes in studying Schwartz' classic. I won't be necessarily separating his text from my own. I may or may not set off his text in quotes or with other emphasis. This is to make the book as readable and usable for you as possible.

While Schwartz set these down, the ideas themselves are universal and may be found in earlier texts.

This is a review, not a book of excerpts. The reason is to bring these principles to life again, to make them available for your success.

This book doesn't follow Schwartz' original structure. It is a study aid. I've rearranged his concepts (slightly) in order to make more logical sense of it. This review is no substitute for reading and studying his original book.

(You've been warned...)

How to Study This Book

It was a find of one of <u>Gary Halbert's old newsletters</u> which led me to find this book and bring it to you.

As someone wise beyond his years, Halbert pointed out that humankind hasn't noticeably changed as to their reactions and motivations – it was still the old classics, based on real testing, which give the core data you need to study.

This book was right up there with "Tested Advertising Methods" by John Caples, "How to Write a Good Advertisement" by Victor Schwab, and "Scientific Advertising" by Claude Hopkins.

At the end of that list, he said to burn anything else. Really. (And it wasn't his advice, but Hopkins'.)

Because you only need the basics. You can work everything else from that.

In my other studies of current "legendary" copywriters (and self-proclaimed experts) I've found that they are all standing on the shoulders of these giants – every thing they say has already been said before. The newer books just have modern words, like the way we talk now.

(The worst among them don't even credit those who've gone before – or put some other special "spin" on rules, laws, and principles these earlier authors found by intensive and lengthy testing. Then it's even harder to learn...)

This is the reason I did all this research to bring Schwartz unique take on age-old principles back to the light of day.

The reason is, again, to get this to you in a format you can use. Starting now.

The steps to take to study this follow Halbert's advice:

> 1. Read the classics (now available in the Masters of Marketing Secrets series) once through, each.

> 2. Then go back through and make your notes. If you like the hardcopy versions, then dog-ear the pages and underline or highlight (or both) everything that seems interesting or vital. (You can both digitally bookmark or highlight otherwise.)

3. Spend some time each day copying the truly great ads by long-hand. This will enable you to learn by doing, to absorb the text on a personal basis.

4. Blog about your findings, or write your own book. Teaching someone is a long-proved method of study. Write it all out as if you have a very attentive student in front of you – and keep them interested as you go.

5. Then go back and study these classics through once again – you'll see more the third time and every subsequent time after that.

Those 5 steps will put you right on the road to success.

Good Luck.

Introduction

In the very beginning of his book, Schwartz lays out the premise and breakthrough within the few pages of its introduction:

"Therefore I've written this book – not from the mail order perspective alone – but from the universal problem of all copy writing: *How to write a headline – and an ad that follows it – that will open up an entirely new market for its product.* An ad that will give a new product immediate profit: that will give an old product a brand-new slant; that will give a competitively-battered product a new weapon – not only to protect itself against its imitators but to actually damage or destroy the loyalty of their following.

"These objectives cannot be achieved by following somebody else's formula – no matter how successful it was for them. they demand creativity they demand a brand-new headline; a brand new approach to the market: a literal advertising "breakthrough." Hence the title of this book.

"This, then, is a practical book, of practical rules that produce, and exploit, creativity, and that are meant to pay off on the very first ad.

"*In copy writing there are the hopes and fears and desires of millions upon millions of men and women, all over the world.* And the copy writer does not create the desire of millions of women all over America to lose weight; but he can *channel that desire onto a particular product,* and make its owner a millionaire."

The key point Schwartz makes here is the one which is driving Internet Marketing as a subject down into a very deep hole:

- There are millions if not billions of variations of the basic human desires.
- As forces, no two are exactly alike.
- While it is simpler to think of these in terms of a few, realize that for every niche, they have subtle variations which have to be discovered and channeled onto your product.

Schwartz explains:

"And the same advertising appeal, that builds an industry in reducing (weight loss), collapses completely when applied to health foods, even though both advertisements may reach exactly the same audience.

"Why? *Because no formula works twice.* Each and every formula is simply the written solution to a particular problem that occurred in the past. Change even one part of that problem, and you need an entirely different formula. That's why... rewriting somebody else's headlines won't make you a copy writer.

"What will work? Innovation, of course. Continuous, repeated innovation. A steady stream of new ideas – fresh new solutions to new problems. Created – not by the impossible route of memory – but by analysis.

"And what is analysis? Analysis is the art of asking the right questions and letting the problem dictate the right answers. It is the technique of the break-through. And it can be learned – just as surely as grammar, mathematics or spelling.

"The first part of this book is about analysis, applied to the profession of copy writing. Its basic thesis is this:

"Every new market – every new product – every new advertisement is a fresh new problem that never existed before on the face of this earth."

Most Internet Marketing simply tells you how to build a sales page by using swipe files. What they don't tell you is that these sales pages only work on certain types of customers and are becoming less and less effective overall.

When all you have is a single hammer, every problem is a nail needing your one solution. "Breakthrough Advertising" gives you a complete toolbox of tools.

Why do you need more than a single formula? *People are wising up* as they visit more and more sites. It's become the buyer's market, not the sellers. One explanation of this likens these two styles as the difference between a harpoon or a net.

"One school hammers the reader with red headlines, yellow highlighting, and aggressive copy that grips the reader like a terrier shaking a squirrel.

"The other school develops a compelling personal voice, nurtures a relationship with the reader, and uses soft-sell techniques to nudge the reader down the path to purchase."

Schwartz' use of analysis says you could actually use either style, but the key point is to do your research to begin with – and find what your customer actually wants. You will be finding the key desire and then honing your copy to encourage and promote your product or service as the solution to that desire.

For those of us who simply do not like ads (and block them) this opens a wide door to get our product or service known and acquired by our targeted clients. We know we have to do marketing, but reject what we've been told is the *only* way to do this. So now we break this logjam.

Moral:

Analysis is the key, not just a hack "formula" that everyone uses.

What the *Copywriter* Needs to Know

A. *Copywriting Basics*

Copywriter's needed attributes:

1. *Ability to analyze a market:*
   - its stage of awareness
   - its stage of sophistication
   - the driving emotional forces that created that market
   - the potential for sales

2. *A Ready Intuition*
   - sense a trend at its start,
   - gauge its force and direction,
   - determine the precise moment it becomes profitable

3. *Verbal Creativity*
   - Give a name to the still undefined,
   - capture a feeling, hope, desire, fear in words
   - create a catchword or slogan
   - focus emotion and give it a goal

Copywriting techniques are directed to the one end of building conviction, instilling the desire for your product and strengthening that desire with the belief that the product will do what the prospect wants.

VERBALIZATION - increasing headline impact

1. strengthen the claim
2. make the claim new and fresh again
3. help the claim pull the prospect into the body of the ad

Personality

Every product, store, or group of products has a distinct and complete personality to the consumer. The personality is complex, with many traits. One of these traits will always be the most effective in summarizing and expressing this personality.

The personality is simplified, symbolized, and sharpened to grasp the reader.

Prevention Headlines

Work when you enable the prospect to imagine those problems afflicting his loved ones, friends, wife and children, even his nation.

Splinter Markets

Markets are not all in one piece. There are different mechanisms that apply to subsets of a market.

Smaller segments can be targeted, regionally or by sociology.

Focusing that appeal then affects all the parts of the campaign - selection of media and channels of distribution. When successful, that campaign can be expanded.

Inside Your Prospect's Head

After the headline, your body copy does the selling. By altering your prospect's vision of reality. Your product emerges as the fulfillment of the dominant desire that caused this prospect to respond to your headline.

You need to take as much copy as you need to accomplish

a. building her desire for that product,

b. make her feel both comfortable and complimented by that product, to visualize the new life structure she's built with that product in it,

c. compensate for existing prejudices and beliefs.

B. How to align mass desire onto your product.

Permanent forces have

1. Mass Instinct
2. Mass technological problem (lack of ease)

The forces of change are:

1. *The beginning, the fulfillment, and the reversal of a trend.*
2. *Mass Education.*

The copywriters job:

1. His first job therefore is to detect already-existing mass desires – inventory them – chart their force and direction.
2. His second job is to harness his products onto their backs.

Your ad (headline) leads your market to your product.

How to create the ad/headline depends on:

1. What is the mass desire that creates this market? (Which we have already discovered.)

2. How much do these people know today about the way your product satisfies this desire? (Their State of Awareness.)

3. How many other products have been presented to them before yours? (Their State of Sophistication.)

I. Choose the most powerful desire that can be applied to that product.

Each mass desire has

- Urgency, intensity, degree of demand
- Staying power, degree of repetition, inability to get satiated.
- Scope - number of people who share this desire.

II. Acknowledge that desire, reinforce it, offer means to satisfy - in a single headline statement.

III. Show the prospect how the product performances satisfy that desire.

Analysis Of Your Product

Any product has the physical product (features), and the product in action (benefits.)

- Price
- Quality
- Continued performances
- Sharpen the reader's mental picture of that performance
- Give a fresh new basis for believability

While any ad can feature one of a dozen built-in product performances, it can only effectively tap into one mass desire at a time.

It is the performance of your product, satisfying the mass desire of your market, that provides the selling power of your ad.

Readers are preoccupied and will only give your headline a single glance - only one thought can penetrate that reader's indifference during that glance. *If your first thought holds him, he'll read the second. If that holds him, he'll read the third - and then probably read through the rest of the ad.*

It's the copywriter's job to get the prospect to read the *whole* story.

C. What Your Prospect's State of Awareness Demands From Your Headline

1. Most are aware of it

Prospect knows of the product, knows what it does, knows she wants it. Ad simply states the name, a bargain price (and how to get it now.)

2. Knows of the Product, but doesn't want it.

Your headline must

a. reinforce your prospect's desire for your product

b. sharpen her image of how your product satisfies that desire

c. extends her image of when and where your product satisfies that desire

d. introduces new proof of how the product satisfies that desire

e. announces a new mechanism in that product which satisfies that desire even better

f. announces a new mechanism in that product which eliminates former limitations

g. or completely changes the image of the mechanism of that product, to remove it from competition of other products (which claim to satisfy the same desire.)

3. Introducing New Product

The prospect either knows, or recognizes immediately, that he wants what the product does; but he doesn't yet know' that there is a product – your product – that will do it for him.

- Name the desire and/or its solution in your headline.
- Prove the solution can be accomplished
- Show the mechanism for that accomplishment is contained in your product.

4. Introduce Products that Solve Needs

The prospect has – not a desire – but a need. She doesn't see the connection between the fulfillment of that need and your product.

- Dramatize the need,
- Get the prospect to realize how badly she needs the solution.
- Present your product as the inevitable solution.

5. Open up a Completely Unaware Market

Each of these stages is separated from the others by a psychological wall. One side is indifference, the other side hold intense interest. A headline that works in one market in one stage of awareness won't work in another market in another stage of awareness. And it won't work in a market once that market moves to a new stage of awareness.

In an unaware market,

a. Price means nothing.

b. The name of your product means nothing.

- c. A direct statement of what your product does, what desire it satisfies, or what problem it solves - simply won't work.

What you are doing essentially in this fifth stage is calling your market together in the headline of your ad. You are writing an identification headline. It echoes an emotion, an attitude, a satisfaction that picks people out from a crowd and binds them together with a single statement.

You tell them what they are, defining them for themselves. You are giving information they need and want, about a problem so vague you are the first to put it into words.

The headline in this case simple sells the remainder of the ad itself. Your prospect must identify with your headline before she can buy from it. It must pick out the product's logical prospects - and reject as many people as it attracts.

In effective advertising, styles change while strategy doesn't.

Desires still exist.

A Final Word on Style in Advertising Copy

Markets change; desires change; fashions change. And so do the acceptable styles of advertisements change. Certain advertising styles – the form your advertising message takes – grow tired with time – then stale – then actually laughable.

When a new style is born, people believe it, and it reinforces the message it is carrying. When that same style grows trite, people cannot see the message for the advertisement.

In effective advertising, though styles may change, strategy does not.

D. Know the Stages of Sophistication of your Market

First in the Market

Be simple, direct, state either the need or claim in your headline. Dramatize that need in your copy as powerfully as possible, then bring in the product and prove that it works.

Second in the market

If the direct claim is still working, copy that and enlarge on it. Outbid your competition.

Third Stage

The market has heard all the claims and their extremes. Mere repetition or exaggeration won't work any more.

Get a new mechanism to make the old promise work. The emphasis shifts from what the product does to how it works. Performance becomes dominant.

Fourth stage

Promise more benefits than any competitor. A new mechanism must be created, but must be believable and significant by your market. Eventually, all these tire your market prospects - they've heard it all. Competitors start dropping out like flies.

Fifth stage

Bring your prospects into your ad through identification, not desire.

E. The 7 Basic Techniques of Breakthrough Advertising

The three dimensions of thought and feeling:

1. Desires

These are the wants, needs, cravings, thirsts, hungers, lusts, etc. that drive your prospect through life. They are *physical* – such as the desire to be thin, or strong, or healthy, or free from acne, corns, bad breath or what have you. they are *material* – such as the desire to possess money, or a big car, or a beautiful dress. they are *sensual* – such as the thirst for a cold glass of beer, or the need for a tired body to stretch out on a soft bed.

2. Identifications

These are the roles your prospect wants to play in life, and the *personality traits* he wants your product to help him build, or project.

These longings for identification – longings for a sharply-defined personality – longings for social status – are, of course, not material] or physical or sensual at all. they complement and intensify the physical desires – add another dimension to them – by making each purchase serve a double duty.

3. Beliefs

These are the opinions, attitudes, prejudices, fragments of knowledge and conceptions of reality that your prospect lives by. This is the world of emotionalized reason that he inhabits – the way he accepts or rejects facts and builds up his universe, the types of thinking he uses to arrive at decisions, the ideas and values which give him comfort and which he believes are permanent and true.

But – important as they are – desire and identification alone are never enough. By themselves, they can never produce the full reaction the copy writer must have if he is to achieve the maximum success with his product. No matter how intense the desire. no matter how demanding the need to identify, both these reactions must be fused with a third great emotional force – Belief

— before they can produce the final overwhelming determinant of action — Absolute Conviction.

It is this fusion of desire and belief — this conviction — this certainty — this feeling in the prospect of being right in his choice — of being assured of what he has been promised — that the copywriter seeks as his ultimate goal.

I. Intensification

The art of salesmanship is expanding existing desire - among more and more people, sharpening it and magnifying it, building it to such a pitch that it overcomes obstacles of skepticism, lethargy, price - and results in the sale.

Advertising is salesmanship in print - the literature of desire, society's encyclopedia of dreams. Advertising gives form and content to desire, providing it with a goal.

Desires are indistinct, and so have only a fraction of their true potential power. Your job is to fill these vague desires with concrete images, to multiply their strength by number of satisfactions that you can suggest to achieve them.

The copywriter uses imagination and enthusiasm to script the prospect's dreams. Chronicle his future and show him in minute detail all the tomorrows that your product makes possible. Translate unformulated desire into one vivid scene of fulfillment after another. The sharper you can draw your pictures, the more your prospect will demand your product and less important will seem your price.

Different media will need different approaches - with the strict limits of text, you either have to boil down projections and images into a few words, or run repetitive instances as a campaign with embellishments through a series of ads.

Your prospect will take only a single dominant image from your ad. Every new way you can present that idea, it becomes sharper and more real and builds more emotional weight.

The opposing forces are the material presented by similar products in other ads, as well as your own phraseology. Repeating the same phrases will bore the prospect - you must vary your viewpoint in subsequent descriptions. You can't repeat, but you can reinforce.

This is *Intensification*. It has several techniques:

1. **Your First Presentation of Your Claims**
Present the product or the satisfaction it gives directly by a detailed description of the appearance or the results it gives.

2. **Put the Claims in Action**
Expand the image - put the product into action for your reader. Show the benefits it gives the reader.

3. **Bring In the Reader**
Put the reader into an action story, a verbal demonstration of what will happen the first day she owns that product.

4. **Show Him How to Test Your Claims**
Have the reader visualize herself proving the performance of your product - gaining its benefits immediately - in the most specific and dramatic way possible.

5. **Stretch Out Your Benefits in Time**
Expand the reader's vision further into time, showing a continuous flow of benefits

6. **Bring In an Audience**
Bring other actors into the scene - testimonials of new perspectives to see the product through.

7. **Show Experts Approving**
Bring in excited experts. But not only celebrities and ordinary people can be used to reaffirm the product benefits.

8. **Compare, Contrast, Prove Superiority**
Competition can be brought in as contrast, showcasing your advantages.

9. **Picture the Black Side, Too**
Get naked - examine your products faults and meet these objections.

10. **Show How Easy It Is to Get These Benefits**
Variations are endless - price, availability, ease of use, durability, even un-boxing it - these give fresh perspectives to reemphasize its benefits.

11. Use Metaphor, Analogy, Imagination

There are infinite opportunities for the use of imagination to present those facts in more dramatic form, outside of the rigidly realistic approach.

12. Before You're Done, Summarize

Summarize - create a catalog of specs. Or a catalog of perspectives (desires) you've presented.

13. Put Your Guarantee to Work

Call for action, with a last brief summary (PS) and guarantee.

II. Identification

How To Build A Salable Personality Into Your Product

The second kind of desire could be titled the Longing for Identification. *Your prospect desires to act out certain roles in his life, to define himself to the world around him, to express the qualities within himself that he values, and the positions he has attained.*

1. Turn your product into an instrument for achieving these roles.

2. Turn that product into an acknowledgement that these roles have been achieved

Every product should offer fulfillment of a physical want or need - and offer him a particular method of fulfilling that need: that defines him to the outside world as a particular kind of human being.

Two Kinds of roles

A. Character roles

Your product helps the prospect in the *constant search for self-definition*, but helping him achieve mastery of his chosen character roles - and secondly help *simplify, condense, or speed up this mastery*. Thirdly, it can serve as *a symbol of that mastery* to invoke acknowledgement or admiration of his friends.

These character roles go beyond the physical satisfactions of the product itself. An extra incentive. The roles are not created by society, but only hinted at - implied and prompted - never measured, ambiguous. Most important - they are subject to fantasy. They are not stated or discussed, but subtly expressed in symbols and images. The prospect doesn't define them to himself or test them against the outside world to see if they are actually true.

So your prospect is more likely to believe in the character roles you assign to him, than he'll believe in your product performance claims or the achievement roles it offers. There is no direct test, no proof needed. Acceptance is easy, painless, non-demanding. Performance claims always require proof. Achievement roles have to stand up to our daily harsh reality. Ease-of-acceptance and consolation-without-cost features give it the strength to supplement verbal claims.

B. Achievement Roles

These have to be won and - most of all - displayed. None of these achievements is obvious. Their potential must be first translated into physical symbols of success for everyone around us to see - products we can buy. In America today, we are known - not only by the company we keep - but by the products we own.

Getting married means all sorts of physical products being acquired rapidly. Getting a raise is known as a new car or house furnishings. Becoming CEO may mean a new, bigger home in a swanky new neighborhood.

Our "material personality" defines us to everyone we meet. Status definers.

This comes into play when your product does the same as the competitors and price isn't a factor. The role your product offers will be the difference.

First job is to discover what kinds of character and achievement roles your prospect is ready to identify with your product, which ones she will reject, which of the accepted ones are most compelling. Present the chosen roles so that they become irresistible.

But these other products – by far the overwhelming majority of the products you will be given to work with – have no such built-in prestige.

Building identification starts with discovering the built-in personality of the product. It has a primary image, which is acceptable, neutral, or negative. Emphasize it or tone it down (if negative.)

1) Subordinate it while you retain it

2) Use as a logical link to bring in more favorable images. Only limit to new images is that you must include the primary image as its base - they must be logically consistent with it's broadest meaning.

Multi-image symbols broaden the size of the market by grafting on new emotional appeals, and to deepen and intensify it's emotional attraction already felt.

Answer these Questions:

1. What do people already believe about the personality of your product?

2. What other primary image do I have to use as a believability-bridge to connect what my prospect already believes with what I want him to believe when he finishes my ad?

Search for image-sources in the physical product:

    1. Its appearance;

    2. Its components and structure; and

    3. The technical background from which it emerged

III. Gradualization (Induction)

How to Make Your Prospect Believe Your Claims Before You State Them

Three Dimensions of the Mind: Desire - Identification - Belief

The need to believe – and the need for secure beliefs – is just as powerful an emotional force as the strongest desire for physical satisfaction, or the most urgent search for expression.

The basic rule of belief, then, can simply be stated as this:

If you violate your prospect's established beliefs in the slightest degree – either in content or direction – then nothing you promise him, no matter how appealing, can save your ad.

But, on the other hand, and even more important:

If you can channel the tremendous force of his belief – either in content or direction – behind only one claim, no matter how small, then that one fully-believed claim will sell more goods

than all the half-questioned promises your competitors can write for all the rest of their days.

As far as advertising is concerned, then, belief is immutable. But it has its function – and one of its great sources of strength – to extend them. Build a bridge between those facts as they exist in your prospect's mind and those they must believe to accept your claims.

This process of leading logically through a gradual succession of more remote facts is Gradualization. (Inductive Reasoning/Marketing.)

The Architecture of Belief

Every claim, every image, every proof in your ad has two separate sources of strength -

> 1. The *content* of that statement itself; and

> 2. The *preparation* you have made for that statement – either by recognizing that preparation as already existing in your prospect's mind, or by deliberately laving the groundwork for that statement in the preceding portion of the ad itself.

We can strengthen the power of each of these statements in two separate ways -

> 1. By increasing the intensity of its content

> 2. By changing the place or position or sequence in which that statement occurs in the ad

Start your ad with an accepted statement, then build a chain of following acceptances on this first one. When a power-claim headline doesn't work – for reasons either of Awareness or Sophistication – they immediately split it against a second head, with far fewer claims in it, but far more likely to be believed. Then they build a belief bridge from this second headline, to the same exact claims they had featured in the first, but now anticipated by careful preparation every step along the way.

> 1. The introduction of the product claim itself – may be made far more effective if it is delayed till the prospect has been prepared to accept it. And

2. This willingness to believe without question-can gradually be built up, layer by layer agreement by agreement, by use of the proper structure.

Belief ultimately depends upon structure. Just as desire depends upon promise, so belief in that promise depends upon the amount of preparation that promise has been given before your reader is asked to accept it.

Strengthen Believability Structure

One fully-believed promise has ten times the sales power often partially-believed promises. Instead of just piling on more promises, strengthen the believability-structure of the original promise.

1. **The Inclusion Question**: permit the prospect to immediately identify with your story.

2. **Detailed Identification**: detail symptoms or problems that are your prospect's reasons for desiring your product.

3. **Contradiction of Present (False) Beliefs**: used to prepare a foundation for strong claim-statements that the reader might never accept raw.

4. **The Language of Logic**: They are the words we use when we reason.

5. **Syllogistic Thinking**: you prove that your product works, through the mechanism of logical reasoning.

6. **Other Belief Forms**:

- *Contingency Structures* – such as "If... then ...", or "Was your., then "
- *Repetition of Proof:* Echoing – such as "These experts found.... These experts found..... These experts found. ..."
- *Promise – Belief – Promise Variation*. Where every sentence of promise is followed (ideally) with another of proof, or verification, or documentation. So that the reader never has the breathing space to question.
- *Paragraph Parallelism*. Where the same word structure used in an accepted statement is then picked up exactly, and used to borrow acceptance for a fresh claim.

There are many more, of course. Some are words, some are chains of reasoning, some are merely the physical arrangement of the copy on the page

IV. Redefinition

1) The product which sounds too complicated. Simplify.

2) The product which is not important enough. Redefine - broaden the benefits of the product.

3) The product costs too much. (above others in its class.) Mechanize - compare it to some other, more expensive standard. (apples vs. oranges)

Notice how similar Gradualization and Redefinition are. Notice how each operates below the surface of the conscious mind. Gradualization by its structure – by its arrangement of facts and phrases. Redefinition by its rearrangement of perspective.

Each is an extremely subtle and powerful way of building belief. Each deserves much more study than we can give it in this book.

V. Mechanization

Demands by the prospect:

1. Demands for more information, more image, more desire. "Tell me more."

2. Demands for proof. "Oh yeah? Who says so?"

3. Demands for a mechanism. "How does it work?"

Stage One: Name the Mechanism

You may now take advantage of their investment by simply naming the mechanism, and going on to beat them with your price or other features.

Stage Two: Describe the Mechanism

1. Because the prospect doesn't understand their mechanism And

2. Because everybody else has the same mechanism, and the same promise, and the same price.

So you have the classic situation of Promise – Reason why.

The first rule of mechanism copy is that it is not scientific discourse. You must never allow it to become dull, or merely factual. You must load it with promise, load it with emotion.

Stage Three: Feature the Mechanism

- If people assume that they know how your product works, sum up in a word or a phrase.
- If people are not quite sure how it works, describe the mechanism until they believe you.
- If you have an exceptionally strong or dramatic mechanism then sell hell out of that mechanism.
- Our readers do not always believe the truth when we tell it to them.

VI. Concentration

Superiority of promise - dealing with competition.

As you know, in the final analysis, no successful copy ever sells a product. *It sells a way of satisfying a particular desire.* And its power to sell ultimately comes from the intensity of that desire.

Several different ways of beating competition:

First, of course, is superiority of product.

Second – superiority of promise.

Third – the product-role.

Fourth – we have response and reaction as a competitive force

And *Fifth* – direct attack – concentration: this careful, logical, documented process of proving ineffectual other ways of satisfying your prospect's desire. *If you can only attack another product – without showing at the same time, by comparison, how your product provides what the other lacks – then say nothing at all! Never attack a weakness unless you can provide the solution to that weakness at the same time!*

VII. Camoflage

How To Borrow Conviction For Your Copy

First is Format.

Second is adopting phraseology.

Third avoids advertising language (which produces a counter-reaction)

    a) Understatement

    b) Deadly Sincerity

Four processes that determine position in your ad:

    1. *Gradualization* – the development of a stream of acceptances from your reader to your statements, leading finally to an inevitable demand on the part of that reader for your product.

    2. *Redefinition* – the removal of preconceived objections on the part of your prospect toward your product, by providing him with a new definition of that product.

    3. *Mechanization* – the verbal proof that your product works – that it does what you say it does.

    4. *Concentration* – the verbal proof that other alternate products do not do this essential function as well.

F. Additional copywriting skills: Verification - Reinforcement - Interweaving

We started this book with the idea that there was a definite technique that could produce better *headlines* than the ones you were using yesterday. And, since the headline is so vitally important to the success or failure of your ads, we devoted the first part of our book to this creative search.

Then, in the second part, we investigated the equally important problem of how to *exploit* that headline. How to lead the prospect from the feeding of interest and curiosity that your headline had aroused in him, into a constantly mounting conviction that *this product* has what he wants, and that it is absolutely capable of giving it to him.

You use body copy to accomplish this second objective – perhaps a lot of it, perhaps very little. In either case, we've examined the three interlocking paths by which this effective demand is created: first, the intensification of *desire*; then the creation of an acceptable product personality or role with which the prospect will want to *identify*; and then the rather abstract structure underlying your copy arrangement that produces believability of your story.

So now we've seen how to reach out to your prospects mind on all three emotional levels: Desire ... Identification ... and Believability.

Now, as our last problem, *we have to put all these elements together*. We have to take all these promises, these images, these devices, these structures – and weave them together into one cohesive unit, that holds your prospect's attention from beginning to end.

In other words, having broken down the ad to analyze the elements that make it work – we now have to deal with the reverse problem: tying it together once again.

Documentation is any sort of proof – statistics, facts, tests, etc. – that your product works.

Mechanization on the other hand is the verbal and logical demonstration, and thus also proof, that your product works.

Verification – which is different from both of them – is the process of arranging your documentation within your copy so that it gains the greatest immediate acceptance from your reader, and has the greatest emotional effect on him.

Reinforcement – How to Make Two Claims Do the Work of Four – If you employ it skillfully, then the impact of one emotion, plus the impact of a second emotion, will often add up – non-mathematically – to the impact of FOUR emotions.

Interweaving – How to Blend Emotion, Image and Logic Into the Same Sentence

The first rule of all copy, of course, is that it produce an emotional impact. As we have seen, over and over again, even in believability copy, even in documentation, every word must carry image, picture, feeling. Weave together your promise, your logic, your emotion, your image. Pack your sentences full of every one of them. Make them blend into each other, till its almost impossible to pull out the individual threads of the rich pattern of conviction and desire you're weaving.

Sensitivity – How to Give Your Reader What He Demands Step In Step Throughout the Copy – Here you are relying on your own powers of empathy You must be, at the same time, not only the writer of your ad but its reader. You must anticipate that point in the copy flow-as it is transformed into a series of impressions in your readers mind where he is going to say: "I've read enough about this. Give me this instead."

And then you must shift the direction of the copy to meet his new direction of interest.

Momentum – How to Draw Your Reader Deeper and Deeper Into Your Copy

There are two types:

  1. Actual momentum phrases; and

  2. Incomplete statements, or teasers, that draw the reader further into the copy in order to complete them.

In other words, YOU are continually throughout the copy:

  1. Creating interest in a specific point;

  2. Raising a question in his mind about that point; and

3. Implying an answer to that question later in the copy.

Mood – How to Pack Your Copy With Drama, Excitement, Sincerity or Any Other Emotion You Wish

- Words and rhythms
- Mood-building

What Are the "Mass Desires?"

Various people have different explanations for these. There are literally an infinite variety of names to call them. This doesn't mean that the emotions themselves are any but a few. The trick is to find authorities who have done the honest research into humankind's actual emotional legacy.

I've narrowed them down to 3 authors who have studied these with no profit to make by teaching copywriters and marketers. They are also not academics, but have actively worked to solve humankind's problems.

Most of the rest of descriptions I've found are marketers selling to marketers – which is also compared to the "blind leading the blind."

Again, the bulk of these descriptions are metaphors. What you call them is up to you. Your research will show you what is the actual strongest desire to use. And your conversations with your audience will tell you how they call it and refer to it.

The below authors – Cialdini, Maslow, and Levenson – have each their own descriptions of how they understand the motivations humankind uses.

6 Key Principles Of Influence By Robert Cialdini

Source: Wikipedia

Reciprocity – People tend to return a favor, thus the pervasiveness of free samples in marketing. In his conferences, he often uses the example of Ethiopia providing thousands of dollars in humanitarian aid to Mexico just after the 1985 earthquake, despite Ethiopia suffering from a crippling famine and civil war at the time. Ethiopia had been reciprocating for the diplomatic support Mexico provided when Italy invaded Ethiopia in 1935. The good cop/bad cop strategy is also based on this principle.

Commitment and Consistency – If people commit, orally or in writing, to an idea or goal, they are more likely to honor that commitment because of establishing that idea or goal as being congruent with their self-image. Even if the original incentive or motivation is removed after they have already agreed, they will continue to honor the agreement. Cialdini notes Chinese brainwashing on American prisoners of war to rewrite their self-image and gain automatic unenforced compliance. See cognitive dissonance.

Social Proof – People will do things that they see other people are doing. For example, in one experiment, one or more confederates would look up into the sky; bystanders would then look up into the sky to see what they were seeing. At one point this experiment aborted, as so many people were looking up that they stopped traffic. See conformity, and the Asch conformity experiments.

Authority – People will tend to obey authority figures, even if they are asked to perform objectionable acts. Cialdini cites incidents such as the Milgram experiments in the early 1960s and the My Lai massacre.

Liking – People are easily persuaded by other people that they like. Cialdini cites the marketing of Tupperware in what might now be called viral marketing. People were more likely to buy if they liked the person selling it to them. Some of the many biases favoring more attractive people are discussed. See physical attractiveness stereotype.

Scarcity – Perceived scarcity will generate <u>demand</u>. For example, saying offers are available for a "limited time only" encourages sales.

Maslow's Hierarchy of Needs

Instead of studying the insane (as Freud and his followers), Abraham Maslow studied the exceptional – those people who accomplished great things. His work is comparable to the 20 years Napoleon Hill spent interviewing over 500 of the greatest movers and shakers of our culture in order to distill his common sense philosophy of success. (Law of Success, Think and Grow Rich)

Source: Wikipedia

Hierarchy

Maslow's hierarchy of needs is often portrayed in the shape of a pyramid with the largest, most fundamental levels of needs at the bottom and the need for self-actualization at the top.[1][9] While the pyramid has become the de facto way to represent the hierarchy, Maslow himself never used a pyramid to describe these levels in any of his writings on the subject.

The most fundamental and basic four layers of the pyramid contain what Maslow called "deficiency needs" or "d-needs": esteem, friendship and love, security, and physical needs. If these "deficiency needs" are not met – with the exception of the most fundamental (physiological) need – there may not be a physical indication, but the individual will feel anxious and tense. Maslow's theory suggests that the most basic level of needs must be met before the individual will strongly desire (or focus motivation upon) the secondary or higher level needs. Maslow also coined the term Metamotivation to describe the motivation of people who go beyond the scope of the basic needs and strive for constant betterment.[10]

The human mind and brain are complex and have parallel processes running at the same time, thus many different motivations from various levels of Maslow's hierarchy can occur at the same time. Maslow spoke clearly about these levels and their satisfaction in terms such as "relative," "general," and "primarily." Instead of stating that the individual focuses on a certain need at any given time, Maslow stated that a certain need "dominates" the human organism.[11] Thus Maslow acknowledged the likelihood that the different levels of motivation could occur at any time in the human mind, but he focused on identifying the basic types of motivation and the order in which they should be met.

Physiological needs

Physiological needs are the physical requirements for human survival. If these requirements are not met, the human body cannot function properly and will ultimately fail. Physiological needs are thought to be the most important; they should be met first.

Air, water, and food are metabolic requirements for survival in all animals, including humans. Clothing and shelter provide necessary protection from the elements. While maintaining an adequate birth rate shapes the intensity of the human sexual instinct, sexual competition may also shape said instinct.[2]

Safety needs

With their physical needs relatively satisfied, the individual's safety needs take precedence and dominate behavior. In the absence of physical safety – due to war, natural disaster, family violence, childhood abuse, etc. – people may (re-)experience post-traumatic stress disorder or transgenerational trauma. In the absence of economic safety – due to economic crisis and lack of work opportunities – these safety needs manifest themselves in ways such as a preference for job security, grievance procedures for protecting the individual from unilateral authority, savings accounts, insurance policies, reasonable disability accommodations, etc. This level is more likely to be found in children because they generally have a greater need to feel safe.

Safety and Security needs include:
- Personal security
- Financial security
- Health and well-being
- Safety net against accidents/illness and their adverse impacts

Love and belonging

After physiological and safety needs are fulfilled, the third level of human needs is interpersonal and involves feelings of belongingness. This need is especially strong in childhood and can override the need for safety as witnessed in children who cling to abusive parents. Deficiencies within this level of Maslow's hierarchy – due to hospitalism, neglect, shunning, ostracism, etc. – can impact the individual's ability to form and maintain emotionally significant relationships in general, such as:

- Friendship
- Intimacy
- Family

According to Maslow, humans need to feel a sense of belonging and acceptance among their social groups, regardless if these groups are large or small. For example, some large social groups may include clubs, co-workers, religious groups, professional organizations, sports teams, and gangs. Some examples of small social connections include family members, intimate partners, mentors, colleagues, and confidants. Humans need to love and be loved – both sexually and non-sexually – by others.[2] Many people become susceptible to loneliness, social anxiety, and clinical depression in the absence of this love or belonging element. This need for belonging may overcome the physiological and security needs, depending on the strength of the peer pressure.

Esteem

All humans have a need to feel respected; this includes the need to have self-esteem and self-respect. Esteem presents the typical human desire to be accepted and valued by others. People often engage in a profession or hobby to gain recognition. These activities give the person a sense of contribution or value. Low self-esteem or an inferiority complex may result from imbalances during this level in the hierarchy. People with low self-esteem often need respect from others; they may feel the need to seek fame or glory. However, fame or glory will not help the person to build their self-esteem until they accept who they are internally. Psychological imbalances such as depression can hinder the person from obtaining a higher level of self-esteem or self-respect.

Most people have a need for stable self-respect and self-esteem. Maslow noted two versions of esteem needs: a "lower" version and a "higher" version. The "lower" version of esteem is the need for respect from others. This may include a need for status, recognition, fame, prestige, and attention. The "higher" version manifests itself as the need for self-respect. For example, the person may have a need for strength, competence, mastery, self-confidence, independence, and freedom. This "higher" version takes precedence over the "lower" version because it relies on an inner competence established through experience. Deprivation of these needs may lead to an inferiority complex, weakness, and helplessness.

Maslow states that while he originally thought the needs of humans had strict guidelines, the "hierarchies are interrelated rather than sharply separated".[5] This means that esteem and the subsequent levels are not strictly separated; instead, the levels are closely related.

Self-actualization

Main article: Self-actualization

"What a man can be, he must be."[12] This quotation forms the basis of the perceived need for self-actualization. This level of need refers to what a person's full potential is and the realization of that potential. Maslow describes this level as the desire to accomplish everything that one can, to become the most that one can be.[13] Individuals may perceive or focus on this need very specifically. For example, one individual may have the strong desire to become an ideal parent. In another, the desire may be expressed athletically. For others, it may be expressed in paintings, pictures, or inventions.[14] As previously mentioned, Maslow believed that to understand this level of need, the person must not only achieve the previous needs, but master them.

Later research

Maslow's later research showed a level above self-actualization, which he called self-trancendence.

Per the New World Encyclopedia:

Self-transcendence

Maslow also proposed that people who have reached self-actualization will sometimes experience a state he referred to as "transcendence," or "peak experience," in which they become aware of not only their own fullest potential, but the fullest potential of human beings at large. Peak experiences are sudden feelings of intense happiness and well-being, the feeling that one is aware of "ultimate truth" and the unity of all things.

Accompanying these experiences is a heightened sense of control over the body and emotions, and a wider sense of awareness, as though one was standing upon a mountaintop. The experience fills the individual with wonder and awe. He feels one with the world and is pleased with it; he or she has seen the ultimate truth or the essence of all things.

The Nine Motives

by Napoleon Hill

(From "Grow Rich With Peace of Mind")

Everything you do is the result of one or more motives. In various combinations we use nine basic motives.

The seven positive motives are:

1. The emotion of LOVE
2. The emotion of SEX
3. The desire for MATERIAL GAIN
4. The desire for SELF-PRESERVATION
5. The desire for FREEDOM OF BODY AND MIND
6. The desire for SELF-EXPRESSION
7. The desire for PERPETUATION OF LIFE AFTER DEATH

The two negative emotions are:

1. The emotion of ANGER AND REVENGE
2. The emotion of FEAR

In those nine motives you can find the roots of everything you do or refrain from doing.

The Four Wants Which Glue Human Experience Together

Lester Levenson achieved a high personal state out of necessity, after having been told he was going to die in a few weeks – leaving him only his mind to sort out his condition.

After his breakthrough, it took him nearly two decades of study to figure out what he had accomplished. Levenson worked out that there were really holding all the humankind experience in place:

- **Wanting Control**

- **Wanting Approval**

- **Wanting Security**

- **Wanting Separation and/or Oneness**

The Wanting **Control** is often typified by frustration or impatience with people around us, as they simply aren't doing what we want them to do - or vice-versa. Like wanting a slow driver in front of you to speed up, for instance. Or talking to the TV and telling someone how they should change some behavior you noticed them doing.

Wanting **Approval** is a very common scene - popularity contests, or resentment at not being chosen for a team - any of these keep us stuck to behaviors where we are acting to please someone, or that we think others should get our OK before they do anything.

Wanting **Security** is far more basic. And needing to control or get approval is held in place by this. This unease is present with any time we are job hunting, or our position with a company or in life is threatened. Of course, this brings a lot more stress into our lives where we aren't in a peace-time activity. But it can also be the annoyance of a power outage, or bills you have to pay.

Wanting **Separation / Oneness** (also understood as belonging) is ever present, but we are not usually aware of it. Wanting to be part of a group is of course a factor in wanting approval, but more basic. Wanting to "get away from it all" is the reverse - but is very basic. And might be the reason we have to have vacations at all. It's also the point of having people recognize your individuality.

These four wants are themselves held in place by the Fear of Death, which is really the fear of losing one's individuality – which gets into another long study quite beyond marketing. (Just know that most people cannot approach their own fear of death without physical pain and distress.)

Addendum

A talk by Gene Schwartz to Phillips Publishing on Oct 8, 1993 about Breakthrough Advertising

I found this in a pile of giveaway stuff someone had left on the Internet. No copyright (I managed to scrounge up a date) but we can tell that this lecture was a follow-up to the book.

This should give you more application to these outlined notes above.

Breakthrough Advertising Secrets

By Eugene Schwartz

I want to explain what I'm doing here. I have two goals. My first goal is to help you as much as I can.

My second goal is to make myself transparent. This is a mystical experience which we undergo every so often. I don't know whether you've tried it. It's marvelous. If you work with a computer - a good computer, lots of bytes - you can say to the computer, "Solve this problem for me." When it does, you can then say, "Make yourself transparent to me. How did you solve this problem?" Then the computer will then go back every step and show you how it reached its solution.

The computer cannot lie. It doesn't have that circuit built in. We have a very large number of lying circuits built into us. Now what I'm going to try to do is take the lying circuits and move them over here and be transparent. That means I'm going to answer any question, give you all the information I can, completely honestly. And we'll see how that works because that's the only way I can possibly impart anything of value to any of you.

Now, I know you're extremely fine professionals and much of what I say for the first ten minutes is going to be too elementary for you. But I cannot discuss anything unless I go over the very, very, very, very beginning.

Okay. This is a timer. It is the most valuable thing I ever bought in my life. I go nowhere in the world without a timer. Whenever I do anything, I press in "3, 3, 3, 3". That means 33 minutes and 33 seconds. I then press the start button. Now we're going to speak for 33.33 minutes.

Now, why do I do this? Because I don't think anyone can work for a very long period of time without interruption. And if you do, you exhaust yourself too quickly. When a posse used to chase a criminal out West where I come from, Butte, Montana, (very important fact) the horse thief would ride for an hour, and then he'd get off and walk the horse for an hour, and then he'd get on the horse again and ride.

And the posse would ride for an hour behind him, get off the horse and walk an hour, and then ride. Why wouldn't the posse go faster?

Because the horse would be exhausted and drop dead. Okay, your mind has a way of dropping dead on you. So what we do is we give it this 33.33 minutes and this gives us room for inspiration to sneak in.

Okay, that's Number One. Number Two is the fact that I come from Butte, Montana. Now, you've probably come from a lot of different places rather than this particular place. I was very fortunate to be born in Butte, Montana. It's a very small town of 30,000 people. I grew up there. I left when I was 15. I live in Manhattan - I lead an extremely sophisticated life in Manhattan. I try never to lose the Butte, Montana in me. Because the Butte, Montana in me is everybody in this huge country of ours.

Now, I don't know how many of you read the National Enquirer every week. I don't know how many of you go to every film that makes over $100 million and see every one of them. You cannot lose touch with the people of this country, no matter how successful or how potent you are. If you don't spend at least two hours a week finding out where your market is today, you are finished! You will have a career of three blazing years and be finished.

Here's A Summary:

Gene Schwartz's rules of great copywriting are in fact the rules of great marketing and great editorial. And, yes, Schwartz says, these are rules, and I'll expound upon them: Be the best listener you ever met.

Work extremely intensely, in spurts. Never "create"- know the product to the core and combine the details in new ways. Write to the chimpanzee brain, simply, directly.

Channel demand - never sell. Think about what your product "does", not "is"- and demonstrate this.

Make gratification instantaneous. Failing often, and testing big differences, shows you are trying hard enough.

"If any writer has set the tone and style for successfully marketing books to consumers, it is Eugene Schwartz. His packages not only sell millions of books for them, but also provide an inspiring model for everyone. No writer in the business can match Schwartz's energy, intensity, and ability to pile benefits on top of benefits on top of benefits. Two of Schwartz's packages - for Dick Benson's Wellness Encyclopedia and Rodale's Secrets of Executive Success - have an astonishing 299 separate and distinct benefits to the buyer in the former and 237 in the latter."-Denny Hatch

Talk Little, Listen Much

So go and get in touch with your people. Don't lose that.

Talk to every cab driver you meet. Speak to everyone you can. Be the best listener you have ever met. Talk little, listen much. That is your market talking.

You don't have to have great ideas if you can hear great ideas. Marty Edelson is the owner of Boardroom, Inc., which is a business about the same size as yours: $100 million a year. He came to me with $3,500 in his pocket, and I told him I'd have to charge him $2,500 as a copy fee, which embarrassed the devil out of me but didn't bother him at all. And he said, "Okay, what do we do?" And I said, "Well, we can start it right now. I'm gonna sit and I'm going to listen and you're going to talk." He talked about four hours about this crazy concept of having a thing called Boardroom - a newsletter called Boardroom. And I just sat there like you're sitting there right now, taking notes. And when he said things I just took it down.

And about 30 minutes into it he said one sentence. And I took it down, and then we finished. And I said, "Well, thank you." He said, "When can you have the copy for me?" And I said "about two weeks. "He walked out. I went home. My wife takes a long time to make up. While she did that, I wrote the ad. I put in the ad from stern to stern. I couldn't give it to him the same night because he would think it was worth nothing. So I then put it away for two weeks. And in two weeks, I sent it to him and he ran it.

Now, my copy was 70% his conversation. The headline was, "How To Get the Heart of 370 Business Magazines in Just 30 Minutes a Month.

"It was his thing. It was his idea. It was his conception. It w his as vision. All I did was write it out and give it to people. Okay. You must be in contact with your market. You must listen. You must let the ideas come to you. If you don't let the ideas come to you, you're going to rely too much on your own creativity. These are all fundamentals.

The number one rule of success in anything - marketing, football (which I'm going to talk about a lot today), chess, etc. - is work. And it's so funny. It's so easy to say, "Work, work, work, work, work." But I have to emphasize that to you. I was telling Richard that I have a very peculiar life. I live at home. I have no boss. I've never had one since the second year In was in business. In am a West-Coast person who doesn't relate very well to the East-Coast clock, and so every morning In get up about ten and by 10:30 or 11:00, I'm ready to go to work. I work every single day of the week. I work on Saturdays and Sundays, too. I have never had a writer's block, an editorial block, or any other kind of block. I create 12 to 15 mailing pieces a year. I never have any trouble getting started on them. I work between three and four hours a day. I work extremely intensely. I work in half-hour spurts as I've already told you.

I'll tell you how I manage to get the work combined with creativity. It's very simple. And I have about an 85% hit ratio. That means 85% of the ads I write pay out.

The Creativity Is Not In You... Never Mistake That

Now, I am of the opinion that the absolutely most talented copy writer in the world, who doesn't work very much, will be beaten by a copy cub who puts in four times as much work, because the creativity is not in you. Never mistake that. The creativity is in your market and in your product, and all you are doing is joining the two together. And the only way you can get the creativity out of your product and your market is to dig it out.

And the only way you can dig it out is dig it out more than anybody else digs it out.

I'm better, result-wise, than many great copywriters, who are better writers than In am, because In work harder than they do - and In can actually see the gaps in their working. Let me explain that. We have what In call the Super Bowl of copy. In use football metaphors, because they are apt, and In hope everybody here understands them.

If you don't, I'll translate them into other metaphors, but they work very well for me. Take Rodale. I'm not going to talk about Phillips Publishing at all here. You're great, you're sensational; you're one of the greatest companies I've ever seen. I've studied you intensely, but I'm not going to talk about you because I'm going to talk about other experiences so you can relate the other strange experiences to your own and therefore broaden your scope of creativity.

Rodale made $315 million in sales last year. It should come close to $400 million this year. That's just Rodale Books. A very good company. It's done many innovative things, produces excellent books, etc. They hire two copywriters for every single new book they do. The two copywriters are sent the manuscript of the book, and they write ads. (Now, you can call them mailing pieces or anything else. I call everything ads, because I like to use short words.) We then submit the two pieces. They are laid out by Rodale's layout department. They send the copywriters a sort of preliminary layout j - then the artist and I talk about it, fix it up, get it right. It's sort of a Super Bowl because these are the highest-paid copywriters in America.

We all get lots of money. I have done that four times this year so far.

It's not a Super Bowl where it's once a year - it keeps going all the time. And you keep running up against these terribly, terribly, terribly great writers.

To compete in it, I read the Rodale book. Seven hundred pages. Four times. I underline the book so intensely that I get 40 or 50 pages of notes out of those readings. Those notes are then sent out to a secretary and she types up those notes so I get a precise "vocabulary." I then go over the vocabulary and begin structuring an ad. We'll talk much more about that in a few moments. When

In am finished, and I am working on the copy, I know more about the book than the editor who has produced it. Because many times at Rodale, they'll come back to me and say, "This is not correct. This is too exaggerated, and I will say, "In combined something from page 116 with 531" and the editor goes back and he says, "Yeah, okay! It can be done!

Finding Those Hidden Desires

Find your readers' hidden desires. They are hidden, because your reader doesn't want to really talk about them, but they are n the subculture, hidden culture, under-culture of our civilization. That's why you've got to read the things that people buy. Anything that people buy. Vanity Fair. You've got to read Vanity Fair. You won't know what's going on unless you read Vanity Fair, People Magazine, The Weekly World News. I don't know whether you are advocates of the Weekly World News. You've got to read that because it shows the extent of people's ability to believe.

When you start working on the project, you go to the person who has initiated the project and you listen. You listen two ways. A person in books and publishing has probably done a lot of words on paper, so you read those. And then, if you can, you sit down with him and you just kind of turn on the tape recorder and you listen, listen, listen.

Nobody's going to know more about it than you. Then you listen to people every single day of your life. You're paid to listen. It's a very bad profession. Very lonely profession. Because it gives you almost no chance to brag or talk about yourself. You really listen. Martin Edelson gave me a headline and theme for a whole new series of books which we have not even prepared yet because he said something at lunch the other day.

You listen, you pick up ideas from people. That's where they are. If you get them talking, they will come out. Know The Product To Its Core Because I have to know that product right down to its core in order to get every single sales appeal out of it, I work harder, and therefore I make 85% winners. Okay, I guess the best guys are much better writers than I am. I'm not really that good. I haven't got their flair. Jim Punkre's a hundred times better than I am. So you work. You work, you work, you work. You leave nothing out. No step undone.

What the client gives you may be inadequate. If it is, you challenge the client. You have no client but the audience. You really don't care about anything but the market or the process. When I'm finished I send my copy in, he sends his copy in, she sends her copy in, whoever it is.

The ads run. Direct mail pieces are mailed out. And I get a report back from Rodale and they say, "You out pulled Jim Punkre 146% on one ad, and he out pulled you 31% on another." You then get his copy, his mailing piece as well as your mailing piece. You then go over in great detail his approach and compare it with your own approach. It's a very good way to learn. Very humiliating. Very enlightening. I can see where they didn't do enough work. I can see where they lost facts.

And the loss of those facts stands out so clearly because I had the facts; they didn't have the facts. Usually, I win. When you are dealing with someone of real brilliance and they do a headline, that's absolutely beyond all belief, then you are going to have a hard time.

Probably you're going to lose then no matter how many facts you have. But nevertheless, 70% of the time if the facts aren't there, they'll hurt you. It's exactly as if you don't have a piece of concrete in your building, and it collapses.

These are fundamentals, but they are universally applicable. If you don't get in the facts, you're just not going to do a top job. When you marshaled the facts, you then begin writing the copy. Now, we are specially privileged people. All of us . Because we are working in publishing. And what is given to you is not a product, but words.

You've got a constant flow of words that you are investigating. So much of your copy is already written for you. So you start with their copy and your comments and additions and inspirations from their copy, and it's there on these 40-some pages. In your computer, on your screen and you start at the very top and you work your way down sentence by sentence and paragraph by paragraph by paragraph. It's very easy.

A Very Simple Way to Make Sure You Get Down to Work

Let's talk about the value of it being easy. Many very brilliant writers - as well as other workers in all fields, physical and especially intellectual - have trouble getting started. They have what is probably known as a writer's block, which is a Western phenomenon and does not occur much in the East. In Zen Buddhism for example, it doesn't occur at all.

Why does it occur here and not occur there? It's very simple. Zen Buddhists about 4,000 years ago invent ed a very simple way to make sure you get down to work. And to make sure you don't have a block.

What happens when a Zen or a, let's say, me - I'm partially Zen - starts to work? What he does is he takes out the piece of copy, and he calls it up on the computer. That is the vocabulary. All those little quotes. He then takes out a cup of coffee. The same cup of coffee every day. He swirls it around and mixes the sugar. Mixes the cream and swirls it around. Then takes out a pad and a pencil and puts it in exactly the same space. He's not doing anything very much. Then he takes out a little timer - that crazy little device - - and punches in 33:33. I've been talking for 13 minutes so far. I know exactly where I am. Okay. He puts in 33 minutes and presses the start button.

When I press the start button, I can do anything I want. All willpower is dissolved. I can do anything I want as long as it relates to the piece of copy in front of me. I can ignore it. I don't have to touch it. I don't have to look at it. But I can't get up from the desk, and I can't do anything except ignore or relate to the piece of copy. I am not trying to write a wonderful ad. I am not trying to earn and extra million dollars. I am not trying to do anything. I have no goal whatsoever as to what that particular piece of copy is going to do for me. All I know is that I'm going to work on the copy, and I have no responsibility to the client, the copy, the prospect, the market, myself and my future except to work.

So finally, after a good deal of looking around - I can't get out of the chair now, I am trapped in that chair for 33.33 minutes, I get bored.

So what do I do? I start reading down the copy! As I start reading down the copy, the copy says to me, "Oh, hey, aren't I beautiful? Why don't you pull me out and put me on top? "Or, "Why don't you change this phraseology? It's extremely ineptly put. Why don't you put it into advertising terminology? "So what happens is that I begin to get into it. And without about five minutes I am working on the copy, making the ad from the copy. Okay. No block, because I am really not doing very much at that time.

Forty pages is a lot. The computer doesn't like 40 pages. New computers like them better - they've got more bytes. But they don't handle them well, and so we are going to have to start subdividing them into categories. The categories are going to become your letter, your flyer, and in a magalog they're going to become one page - the little sidebars in the magalog, etc. So you begin to sort it out, and you begin to get it. As you sort things out into categories, things leap out at you. When they leap out at you, you capture them at that moment.

The computer has a thing called a highlighting device - the bold key - you hit the bold key, and you make them into a headline or a sub-headline. They are the points of contact, the most dramatic points of contact you have with your prospect, with your market.

I hope you can all see this ad. It says, "Burn Disease Out of Your Body. "Crazy. A really wild piece written in 1979. The full, headline is "How Modern Chinese Medicine Helps Both Men and Women Burn Disease Out of Your Body Using Nothing More Than the Palm of Your Hand. "Okay. This ad has been running for 14 years now, selling the book, which sold for $6.95 when it first ran and sells for $33 now. It will sell more copies this year than it ever did before. And we paid the author well over a million dollars. I wrote it as a special favor for the author because he had done a special favor for me - he gave me back the use of my right hand after I had my stroke. I paid $125 for the layout. It's as crude as can be. I never thought the thing would sell.

Layout, letter, very crude, very small type. A lot of violations. We're going to go over this in some degree of thoroughness later on. I couldn't get anybody to run it, so I started my own business to run it.

And there I was.

How Modern Chinese Medicine Helps Both Men and Women BURN DISEASE OUT OF YOUR BODY Using Nothing More Than The Palm Of Your Hand!

"How to treat high blood pressure, bursitis and arthritis - and prevent them from degenerating further, or even reverse them

- simply by massaging the outside of the legs in a downward way. This pose helps reduce water retention and excess weight.....cures and prevents hemorrhoids, and cures problems of the prostate, such as ...enlargement and cancer.

"Eventually throw your glasses away, and never need to see an eye doctor again, simply by rubbing around the eyes for a few minutes every day. "If one has strong..., they never grow old..."

FREE... INSTANT IMPROVEMENT

By applying the ...faithfully, he regulated his bowel movement, lost 40 pounds, and was filled with new energy."

FREE HOW TO RUB YOUR STOMACH AWAY

"In just a few weeks, she had lost five inches in her waist, hi ps and thigh area." MAIL ENCLOSED CARD FOR FREE COPY. I got a call from him...and he told me...that he had already lost...his best. "THE SIMPLEST AND MOST NATURAL WAY TO LOSE WEIGHT IS BY THIS EFFORTLESS TWO-MINUTE EXERCISE."

By such apparently simple means, the superfluous areas of the stomach and abdomen are literally rubbed away.

MAILER: Instant Improvement, Inc.

PACKAGE: Dr. Chang's Book of Internal Exercises

COPYWRITER: Eugene M. Schwartz

FIRST MAILED: 1979 The 9" x 12" outer envelope

Okay. "Burn Disease Out of Your Body Laying Flat on Your Back, Using Nothing More Than the Palm of Your Hand" are not my words. They're the author's words. I wrote seven paragraphs of this letter. But I had the ability to let this man speak for himself. And he still speaks to millions of Americans. We are mailing more in January than we mailed for the first eight years of the mailing. And it goes against very, very strong, strong, strong wonderful copy, including your own copy. And it still continues to do well.

That just about finishes the fundamentals.

After 33.33 minutes happen, this thing goes crazy and rings all over the place. You stop. You push the stop button. You don't do anything from that moment on. If you are in the middle of a sentence you really leave that sent ence go. If you lose it, you lose it. That's too bad. You are under the command of something higher than you. It's so funny to use these metaphors. You pull yourself and push yourself back. You stand up. You now have five minutes of compulsory leisure. You are not to create any more! You are not to work anymore. You have five minutes. Now. Coffee low? We'll have to make a new cup. Dog? Play with the dog. Go shave (if you're a man, of course). Okay. You do something.

You see, you have to do something, but you can't work. You have to engage your mind. You have to engage your intelligence. But you can't engage your mind or your intelligence on what you have been doing.

Why? Because you are about to create. You have been working until that point. Now you are about to create.

How Does One Create?

Now let's talk about creation. How does one create? How does one become creative? How does one get new ideas? How does one solve problems that are intractable and cannot be solved? That you've worked on for weeks and thrown your hands up in despair? Well, that again is quite simple. We'll take a few minutes on this because it's really so valuable, and it's so much a habit that can become cultivated, and then become rather automatic and give you a statistical proportion of hits. That means new ideas, in this case.

Your conscious mind is actually your focus of attention. The conscious mind is absorbed with what you are paying attention to. I'm paying attention to all of you when I'm speaking at this particular moment.

Your conscious mind can only hold about seven memory bytes. That's pretty small, so you have to focus. Your conscious mind is where you focus your attention. It's very narrow. It's wonderful. It's fantastic for working out syllogisms, consequences, etc. It will not create for you.

What is creation? Creation is a lousy word. It's a lousy word that confuses what you really do to perform a simple little procedure.

Creation means create something out of nothing. In the beginning, God created Heaven and Earth. Okay, only God can do that. We can't do that: We're human. So let's throw creation out, and let's talk about connectivity. What you are trying to do is connect things together.

You're trying to practice connectivity. You're trying to get two ideas that were separate in your mind and culture before, and you are trying to put them together so they are now one thought. You want something new to come out, but new doesn't mean it never existed before, it means never joined before. New - in every of discipline - means ne ver joined before.

You've got to trick that conscious mind because that conscious mind isn't big enough to connect all these widespread phenomena. So what you do is you take your conscious mind and you focus it on making a new cup of coffee! That holds it there, and then ideas can kind of bleed into the back of your mind and come into the front of your mind.

The best example is Mozart - a most creative man, who was writing symphonies at six, seven, eight. I don't know whether you saw the movie Amadeus. It shows very truthfully and very well how he wrote.

He never, ever, rewrote. He never changed. He wrote his scores in pen and ink. He never changed a note of them. They were always perfect and the highlight of his genius of course, but that doesn't mean a thing.

How did he do it? Well he did it very simply. He composed at a billiard table. He would stand at the billiard table, and he would have a single white billiard ball. He would have a pen and an inkwell, and he would have the score. And he would take the white billiard ball in his left hand while he had the pen in the right hand and he would throw the white billiard ball out against the three cushions. And it would bounce off the three cushions. It's random, how it comes back, to a certain extent. It never comes back exactly at the same place, so he had to focus on the trajectory of the billiard ball until it came back.

When it came back here or here or here, he had to focus on that hand being at the exact right place. Meanwhile, while his conscious mind was over here, his unconscious mind slipped the note back to him and then he had the next note. Every note was a billiard ball traveling.

Every note was a distraction. Every note was an addition. You've got to break out of that conscious prison to be unconsciously creative, which means to connect unconsciously things that haven't been consciously connected before.

My greatest inspirations or creations come when I'm shaving. I am the poorest shaver. I cut myself continually, and I'm always running back and forth between the bathroom and my desk. They are right next to each other because I have to get it down before it slips away.

I'll draw one of my great connections for you. A very successful ad. It says, "71-year-old man has sexual congress five times a day!"

Problem? This was a sexual health product. There are many sexual health problems and health products around. Everybody constantly talks about super-potency, etc., etc. They all say you can gain back everything you had. How was that going to compete in a market with a very simple, very crude mailing piece?

And I found I could do it by two ways. Number one, I used "sexual congress" which is a very strange way of phrasing this particular act, but which was a very typically American way in the 1890s. And number two, I talked about a 77-year-old man when I'm selling products to 40 - year-old men. I gave the extreme. I did not think of this. I had no idea of thinking of this. It came to me, in fact, when I was shaving. I put it down, and it pulled 9% on the first test!

Okay, those are the fundamentals. Let's go over them again.

The first, most dominant, absolutely incontrovertible and indispensable fundamental is that you work harder than anybody else, therefore you make more money than anyone else. A one -to- one connection. Red Blake - coach of Army, during WWII, a great coach - said the will to win depends on the will to prepare. You gotta prepare. Prepare, prepare, prepare. You got to go over it. And on the sixth reading you'll see the great stuff.

Second is the ability to get to work. If you don't get to work you can't make money. And you get to work simply by using techniques for thinking creatively.

Richard-Stanton Jones: What are some of the techniques you use for tuning in or listening well?

Schwartz: Number one: One hour a day, read. Read everything in the world except your business. Read junk. Very much junk. Read so that anything that interests you will stick in your memory. Just read, just read, just read. Subscribe to Ladies Home Journal Cosmopolitan, Vanity Fair. Get all the very low stuff. Low culture makes big money.

Got to remember that! There is your audience. There is the language.

There are the words that they use.

Remember, when somebody does a picture, about a kid who gets lost over Christmas, and makes $300 million, a lot of people like that! If you have to go to that well not once, but twice, and you have to say to yourself, "What makes this reach these people?

Assume People Are Wonderful

Assume, as your constant assumption, that people are wonderful. You might read Dale Carnegie's book How To Win Friends and Influence People again. That book is one of the greatest books ever written. And everybody should read it every two or three years. The assumption is that everybody you're out there writing to is a good soul. As my father used to say, the sale of the earth. They really want to be nice, honest and successful. They want to be happy. And they want to have friends.

And assume that's there and then see what they're very interested in at this time.

When you are at parties - and this is extremely difficult - listen. Sit down and listen. The technique of listening is extremely simple, and most people - 80% of people - don't really practice it. You look the other person in the eye and you say, "Gee, you're wonderful." You say, "Well, isn't that interesting. What do you do?"" Oh, I'm publishing."

"Who do you work for?" "Phillips Publishing."" Oh, terrific! What do you do there?" And you sit and you listen and you listen and you listen.

And every time they say something, you nod. And memorize specific statements, so you can feed them back to them in the same conversation. In that way, the person goes into a talking frenzy.

He begins to feel very important, very comfortable, very happy and he loves you and he will confide in you. That gives you his inner secrets. I have - pardon me for saying this - but I have had a dinner conversation with a woman I have never met before at which the entire table around us - 12 people - stopped when she said, "I tell you my cervix is no larger than my little fingernail!" This is because people will become hypnotized by their own stories.

Write To The Chimpanzee Brain

All the exposure books. Every single one of them. Barbarians at the Gate. You know, all the ones that said, "These are the way people got away with it." Get that book. Everything that tells you how to be crooked - as an investor I would devour them. People are two-sided. I mean, there are so many ways we can go. You are all chimpanzees.

I've got terrible news for you!

There are three kinds of chimpanzees invented by nature: the regular chimp, the pygmy chimp, and this thing called man. Man was the third. He came along a couple of hundred thousand years ago.

So you have three brains! You have a reptilian brain, a mammalian brain and human brain: the cerebrum up here which thinks logically.

You don't use the human brain that much in reading copy. You really use the chimpanzee brain in reading copy. You are an animal. When it gets you in the gut, what does that mean? It gets you in the chimpanzee brain. That's why you use very simple and very vivid words when you're dealing with investment copy, I think. In any other kind of advertising I've ever run I used very simple words.

Inside of us we have this hidden chimpanzee. It gives us a lot of trouble. But it provides a lot of opportunities for marketers. The person who buys investment material wants to make a lot of money very, very, very fast. He may logically know he can't do that, but he would love to do it. And believe me, he goes home and presses that TV button and sees right in there. That is your junk reading. Now, he's going to look for the best, most rational and most honest approach possible. But he's also going to have that little sly side of him and you are going to have to appeal to that to sell to him.

Copywriting is simple writing

I also just want to quickly throw that into another dimension. I guess you all supervise or work with the copywriters. And you all write copy.

You all speak copy. You're all trying to sell somebody something - if it's only a raise or going out on a date, or having somebody do what you want them to do.

Copy writing - as well as all effective writing - is simple, transparent writing. It is not literary writing. The surest way to know that something is failing as copy is to have someone come in and say,

"God, that was great copy! Oh, I love the ring of that sentence! And that phrase you put in there moved me!" Uh, uh! What happens is that you want them to come in and say, "Jesus Christ, am I in that much danger?" Or, "is there really a way that I can have sexual congress fives times a day?" That's what you want.

You are presenting a showcase for your product. Just like a store showcase on Fifth Avenue. You want the person to be able to look through the copy like the person is able to look through the glass in the showcase and see the product inside. If that glass becomes dirty, reflective, or calls attention to itself in any way, you have failed. If you want to write a novel, go write a novel. And I have! But don't write novel copy!

Simple, dramatic, move-gut copy. There's also enormous room for logical terminology in ads. And you should use it continually. But that is logical, terminology and structure. Don't use hard words in ads - words with more than three syllables - unless you want to give a certain flavor at that moment. You've got to be simple. Remember.

The Headline Does Not Sell

Let's get into specifics. This desk here is a good example of what your table at home looks like every day and what your prospect's table at home looks like every day. Here I come in, and I've had a tough day.

And I'm pretty tired. And I've got one, two, three, four, six, seven, eight, nine or more pieces of mail. What is my movement when I open these pieces of mail? I go this way and this way and this way, okay?

My actual rhythm - and your actual rhythm - is you pick them up like this. You may pick them up like this, and you look. The envelope has ten seconds. You, as a company, as an executive, as a copywriter, have ten seconds. The hand comes up, the hand looks, the hand throws away.

Or, the hand stops. Something gets him. You have ten seconds for your headline to stop that hand from throwing your piece away. So what is a headline? That's very important. And a headline is a very simple device that has a very easy job to do. Except that people make it extremely hard.

The purpose of this headline: "Burn Disease Out of Your Body" - which is the first thing they see in those ten seconds - is to get them to read the next paragraph. That's all it is. Nothing else. It sells nothing. It confirms nothing. It argues nothing. It establishes nothing about the firm. If it stands by itself it would do nothing in the world, but all it's gotta do is, it's got to get them to read the next paragraph.

Second, how long should a headline be? That's a classic question in copywriting. And, of course, the answer is, "No determined length."

The headline depends strictly on how long it gets you to stop the person and get them going.

And the third question is, how many headlines can there be in a mailing piece? And that, of course, is as many as you get on the page and make work.

In the old days, people used to think that there should be one great headline. One super, marvelous headline that was only words - five words, six words, seven words - that would stop, and everything came out of that. The classic example is, "Why Men Crack." It's a great headline - ruled for years. Three words, and that was it! It is represented by this one. "A 71-Year-Old Man Has Sexual Congress Five Times a Day." Then you begin to realize you got all this paper.

You're paying a fortune for all this paper, so why don't you use it in any way you can.

All you want the person to do is pick up the envelope, see what he's got, read it, say, "Umm, that looks interesting - turn it over on the back - there's something on the back - read the back - says, Umm, that looks interesting," and he opens it. So all you're asking him to do is move through your copy. Nothing more. You're not trying to sell.

The headline sells the first line. The first lines sells the second line. The second line sells the third line. And the third line sells the fourth line, etc.

There's a tremendous advantage there. There are things that you can say in the middle of an ad which will be believed because you prepared them for it. But, if you said it at the top of the ad, or in the envelope, it would be thrown away. The guy would say, "This is ridiculous, this is insulting my intelligence, I'm not going on. "If you can get him into the middle, if you can get certain facts to him, then he is prepared to believe. And if he is prepared to believe, he's prepared to buy.

There's a headline. Should it be tremendously big?

Overwhelming? Not really. This is an envelope. Just take a look at it. What it says is, "If a Disease Is as Crippling as This, Then You Certainly Have To Treat It With Drugs. Or Do You? Decide For Yourself From the Startling Facts Below." Well, that's the whole headline. It's pretty much that. If they start reading, "if a disease is as crippling as this," then they will probably finish this. And if they do that they will go on to that. If they do that, they will go on to that, they will go on to that. There must be what, a hundred words here? I don't know. And then you turn around "Is Premature Aging the Most Universal Unconquerable of All the Common Diseases Listed Inside? Not at all. For startling, up-to-the-minute evidence that it is not, see inside!"

Okay, this is a dirty envelope - "ugly, as Richard calls it. This is an ugly layout. I've been driving Rodale crazy for over 15 years giving them this kind of envelope. This sold 50 million (five-zero) million dollars worth of books. That's a lot of books to sell on a single folded piece of paper. Why? Because it reaches out and touches somebody, and they're willing to see and pay for these little miracles.

I wrote this to see how much copy I could get for an envelope on a single piece of typewritten paper single spaced. Then I threw it down to the design department. And what they did is they took the top of it which said, "tricks of the trade so powerful they could change your life." And then we gave 20 of those tricks of the trade right there on the envelope. Right there in the headline. "A form of ordinary water that, by itself, can relieve cold symptoms. Page 273.""Simple, do-it- yourself ways to not only burglar-proof your door, but also have invincible windows. Page 159."

This ran as a control for 15 years. When it finally faded out, they went into this, which is prettier. Because it's on coated stock, in color. And this says, "Old-timer tricks do the impossible around your home." So you've gotta learn that a headline doesn't sell. It has nothing to do with selling.

Who Are You Writing To?

You are not writing to a private person. You are not writing to a bunch of people. You are writing to a number of people who share a private want. Remember that. If they don't share the want, they are of no use to you. If there aren't enough people that share the want deeply enough to spend the fifty bucks for a newsletter or $30 for a book, they are of no use to you.

You are writing to a number of people who share a private want, and you are addressing them as if they were the only person in the world.

What is the most powerful word in advertising? Not "free!" "It's "you!"

And yet so many times you see "these symptoms appear." How about "your symptoms appear?" What you are talking about is you. The person who has got this piece of paper in their hand and is on the other side of your copy. You, you, you, you, you, you, you, you, you.

If it doesn't have the word "you" a hundred times, I really don't like it very much.

Now, when you are writing to a public that shares a private want, they may share subsections of the want. And therefore, what the hooks - the promises - are doing is pulling out a subsection and putting it in.

I'm trying to pick up five percent in this hook, 10% in another hook, etc. And you've got to have an overall way of getting everybody to read through.

Notice that the headline says, "If A Disease as Crippling as This." Well, that includes arthritis victims, bursitis victims, emphysema victims.

Headline Elements: Promise = Intrigue, Mechanism = Emotion

Let's talk about finding the headlines. We're getting very technical now. Very specific. You have your 40 pages of notes. And you are going through your 40 pages of notes. And you begin to see a picture emerging. There was a book that Rodale had a lot of trouble with. And they kid of figured that maybe they shouldn't have published it. It was a book on arthritis. And Rodale is extremely good - the best in the country, I think, at doctor remedies, hidden doctor remedies. And this book went way off from that because it wasn't written by doctors. And, of course anybody that buys Rodale books, buy doctor remedies.

This was a book about people who cured their arthritis by themselves that the doctors didn't really agree with. 766 different people who had different cures which they found by themselves. How are you going to reach them? So the headline is, "Sneaky Little Arthritis Tricks. Natural Foods and Do-It-Yourself Secrets That Pain-Proofed Over 100 Men and Women Like You."

I figured that these people were sneaking around doctors. And they felt guilty about doing it. Nobody said this, incidentally. It isn't in the book. And the people who went to the doctors or the market for this were still in pain. Arthritis is a very intractable disease, and we haven't cured to it yet, even though I hope we will in the next five years. So I thought the only way we could do this was "sneaky little" - both words you don't usually use in advertisements like this.

Now, in this particular case, when we said "Sneaky Little Arthritis Tricks," this grabbed attention. Then what's the next step? - What are they? "Natural Food and Do-it-Yourself Secrets That Pain-Proofed over 100 Men and Women Like You."

Notice how it's step-by-step. You grab their attention; you send them into the mechanism. That is the foods and secrets. You send them into the first reward: pain-proof. Then we have these pictures and all these testimonials one, two, three, four, five, six, seven; there were seven quotes from seven of these 776 people. One says, "I enjoyed a total remission of my arthritis." Another says, "I have not had sciatica since 1971." Another said "All symptoms disappeared and have not returned." Okay. What you've got is intrigue in the first part, a mechanism for giving you something you can't get in the second part, and proof in the third part.

You've also got enormous gut emotion in the envelope because of those exceptional pictures that they put. Look at that beautiful woman at the bottom. You can't help relating to her. Look at the man with the little child kissing him at the top. This is what you want. You have this woman. Look at her stride. Very strong. This is what you want. So you have great promise, intrigue. You have a mechanism - a new mechanism that delivers that promise. You have proof that that promise has been delivered to people like you. And you have deep emotion. That's what you need. All of them combined, get the prospect to read.

How to Uncover Great Headlines

Let's about how we build an ad. I'm going to read you this; this is very successful, the second-longest running direct mail piece.

We start with "How Modern Chinese Health and Medicine Helps Both Men and Women." That is the small type above the headline.

What does that do? In the first place, it establishes the point of difference. They're going to be running to about 150 lists; 150 lists all have their own product. How do you establish a point of difference between this product and their product? Especially when it's a book as old as this one? By talking about Chinese medicine which is ancient, but at the same time it's modern. Most people haven't heard about it, but they're intrigued. We all know how powerful the East is. And both "men and women" is an inclusion headline which looks like an exclusion headline. "Both men and women" means if you're a man you can read this; if you're a woman you can read this. It's very crude, but it works.

Then you go to "Burn Diseases out of Your Body Lying Flat on Your Back Using Nothing More Than the Palm of Your Hand." Why is this effective? Because, of course, you'd like to get rid of disease, but how can you burn disease out of the body? And then the contradiction immediately comes up, "Lying Flat on Your Back Using Nothing More Than the Palm of Your Hand." Again, you're not taking drugs, you're not seeing your doctor, you're not undergoing surgery, etc. This sounds extremely easy. So what you've got is inclusion; a very powerful claim and a very easy mechanism.

Now notice what you have given the reader. You have given a great deal of information in three sentences. And the person is now ready to go on. "This may be the most startling news you've ever read. And we are going to let you prove its merits yourself without risking a single penny. It is that different. They're powerful, they're provocative and controversial."

We are going to let you prove its merits yourself without risking a single penny. Thus the guarantee comes to the front of the piece.

Once you have said "without risking a single penny", it means you, the publisher, are taking a chance on them, the reader, liking your product. Then you can say it is that different, it is that powerful, that provocative and controversial. If you had said at the front without any preparation, "it is that different, that powerful, that provocative and controversial", it would not be believed as readily as if you say, "I'll put my money on it that this will give you these benefits."

Prepare the Ground for Each Claim

What you've done is you've taken a claim and made it powerful by preparing for it. You must prepare. Again, you have the time to prepare because you certainly don't have to sell now. You've got a whole mailing piece to sell. The more time you have, the more you can sell. "Let us explain. The Chinese do not believe in surgery or medicine for major illness. They prevent such illnesses instead with a series of mild, almost effortless internal exercises." What you have been relying on is no longer necessary. Surgery and medicine are expensive, dangerous, and painful. Also embarrassing. But the Chinese don't believe in it. They prevent. Instead of treat, prevent. With a series of mild, almost effortless internal exercises. It sounds like fun!

"If you do not have an open mind, please stop reading here, for this letter's about to introduce you to a new, although it is 4,000 years old, a different type of self-healing. Born in China, over 40 centuries ago, it's called Taoist medicine. And we will let the foremost practitioner of it in the Western world, Dr. Stephen Chiang, gave you a brief and startling introduction to these effortless exercises."

"Brief." "Startling." "Effortless." Look at adjectives. Adjectives are where you carry your emotion. Adjectives are gut words. Adjectives are description words. Adjectives are feeling words. Look at your adjectives. Do an adjective check when you've done your copy. Very important words.

You can say something with adjectives and without adjectives and have absolutely two different things. And then Dr. Chiang comes in, and the rest of the entire mailing piece is quotas from the book.

Except for one or two sections which I am going to get to next.

Now, he makes extremely powerful claims. All of which are exceptionally pleasant. "Clicking the teeth, as shown to you on page 132, will help tighten the joints in the body and keep the teeth healthy." Now how can your teeth help tighten your joints? This is the precursor of Rodale's "Doctors' Home Remedies", in which we gave these silly little things like putting a tea bag up to your eye to improve eyesight. Twist, twist, twist? The more twist, the more powerful.

"The muscles in the abdomen and body will tighten and become toned and strengthened. Excess water and flesh will be eliminated and the belly is shrinking. And you are doing all this with the palm of your hand."

Biography Builds Belief

Once you have claims this powerful, people are going to say, "Isn't that nice? I don't believe a word of it." You can't make powerful claims unless you can prove them. You have to prepare for them, and you have to prove them. You've got to stop them and make them believe.

So what we had which we didn't have in almost any other ad at that time, 14 years ago, was a little section up here in the biography. Got a great, Chinese face. He's 67 years old; he looks about 40. Great Chinese face.

Well, what do we say about him. I'm going to take a few minutes to read that, because it's very important. "Stephen Chiang, Ph.D., M.D. comes from a family which has practiced medicine for more than 400 years. Dr. Chiang's great-grandfather was personal physician to the Empress Chai Chi and the first ambassador to the United Kingdom. Dr. Chiang has a Ph.D. in philosophy, holds two law degrees and received his medical degree from China, from the Yung Chee University Medical School, where he was trained n both Western and Chinese medicine. "

Okay, so we've got his background. Now what has he been doing recently? "Currently he is on the faculty, consulting and conducting classes in Chinese medicine in such universities as University of California, University of Oslo; the United States Health Service Hospital, San Francisco; the University of Oregon; college of San Mateo; Golden West College; center for Chinese Medicine and Continuing Education.

"In addition, Dr. Chiang has given many workshops where..."

I promise you every word of that is read. It's in eight-point print type. It's read, because people want to believe...

You've Got to Demonstrate the Product

Okay, now that you have proof, you've got to demonstrate.

Demonstration and proof are extremely powerful. You do this by saying, "Let us give you the simple internal exercise that energizes the heart. This exercise shows you immediately how incredibly simple, how incredibly easy, how incredibly comfortable these internal exercises are. When you receive Dr. Chiang's book to prove or disprove it at our risk turn immediately, without preliminary reading, to page 140."

Important, because you're going to give something they should do with the book. You don't want them to send it back. And also, it sounds very good. It's convincing them. They are now using the book with you in the letter. There you will be shown the exact way to hold your body while energizing your heart. No movement. We'll repeat. No movement is required. All you do instead is this: sit or stand in a comfortable position with your hands simply extended in front of your chest at the level of your shoulders. Make sure that the fingertips of each hand almost touch. But keep about a quarter of an inch between them. Keep your eyes focused on the top of your fingers. That is all there is to the entire exercise. Nothing else. No further effort. Not even the simplest movement of the body is required. Nothing more.

Nothing more to do. Not a single strain in any part of your body. Your heartbeat doesn't rise a single beat. And yet, what happens is this:

"The exercise creates a flow of energy."

You have just demonstrated the book. You have taken one exercise, one paragraph out of a 270-page book, and you have said to the person, "Get on the floor and try this. Feel what happens. If you don't like what happens, don't send for the book. If you do like what happens, you have already demonstrated the first part of the book and you can now order and can get everything else."

Every Sentence Is a Branch of a Tree The ad is built as a mosaic. Every sentence in the ad is built as a mosaic. First you give a proof. You give a claim. You give a mechanism, which is how the claim is achieved. You give a proof. You give documentation. You give demonstration. Every sentence is a branch on a tree. And the words in the sentence as the leaves on the branch. First the branch comes; that's bare outline of the sentence.

And then you see out of the branch, the leaves popping up. The leaves give the branch color. They give the branch beauty. They give the branch strength and power because they collect the energy coming from inside. That's what you do.

You Channel Demand

I find as a personal phenomenon advertising to be an extremely easy discipline. It can be very hard if you work at it too hard. It can be very easy if you flow along with it. What are you doing when you market something? You are not creating demand for a product. If you think that you are creating demand for your product, you've doomed yourself to a lifetime of hard work and failure. You can't create demand for anything because demand is too large for you to create.

The demand has to be out there. The demand has to exist before you even walk into the picture. Think of yourself as an atomic scientist.

You find a tiny thing called the atom, which has got enormous, enormous, enormous stored-up, locked-in power, and you find that if you take two atoms and bind them together, you can release the power. That's what you're doing.

You've got a market out there that wants security in retirement.

You've got a market out there that wants alternative healing outside of the pain and embarrassment inflicted upon them by the medical profession. But they want the authority of a doctor. What you are doing is you are taking that demand from every one of those persons, individual people, private people who comprise that market. And you are simply turning it or focusing it or channeling it onto your product.

That's all! It's so much easier. If the demand isn't there, no matter how great a copywriter you are, you are going to fail.

You cannot create demand. You can only channel demand. Demand is there. Demand is enormous. The bigger the demand, the better your ad is. You are getting in a boat and letting the stream carry you. Just don't think that you can paddle up against the stream.

The Associative Process

Lorna Newman: I have a question. This comes back to the vocabulary of the list of quotes. When you look at the product, do you only pull the product to make the list or do you add from elsewhere as you go along?

Schwartz: Copywriting, of course, is an associative process. The list becomes an associative stimulus list. And as you go down through the list, you'll get ideas! Okay, you hit the end of bar twice, that gives you a space, and you write it in. Now, you may want to disassociate your own ideas from the quotes, so you can put your ideas in bold, underline, italics, anything else. The more disassociative ideas you get, the more chance you have of getting a stronger ad. But, you will find that authors are not writing copy; they are writing text. Their vocabulary is different, and their entire conception of what it means to write is different.

So you come up with a paragraph about half a page long. A real big paragraph. And you'll see this great idea in there. So make it bold and write a headline. That's a wonderful way to do it. Write a ten-word headline. That makes you condense the thought, and makes you search for advertising terminology to parallel the thought.

When you get through doing that, don't read what you've just written.

It's not worth reading. Just keep going. Now, what you want to do, is get yourself into a creative frenzy. Like a feeding frenzy. You want to get the ideas flowing so thoroughly, that pretty soon you're not condensing what he or she has written, but pretty soon you are coming up with entirely new concepts that will apply.

Here's an example:

You remember Gecko? In "Wall Street"? Let's say that he's kind of burnt in your memory and you're selling an investment letter, and you remember something he said at the trial, on the stock market. And all of a sudden, that idea is floating there, that image, Gecko, and here is the investment letter you're working on. And as you're doing this pulling and condensing headlines out of the text you're given, all of a sudden, you get something from that, and Gecko suddenly joins. It fuses. Like an atomic reaction in your mind. And you have a powerful line to sell your product.

Then, when you're through with everything, go away for a day, and come back. Then, you judge. Always remember, incidentally, that you cannot judge. I've been doing copy now for 35 years. I've sold millions and millions and millions of things. What does my experience allow me to say about the power of an ad? What does your experience allow you to say about the power of an ad before it's run? Absolutely nothing!

You must remember that. You don't know anything about how an ad is going to pull. The only way you can tell is to get a test cell.

I don't believe in focus groups or anything else. I think they're wonderful, but they don't give you an indication. Sometimes the things that they think you should throw away are the things that really go.

Only the test can decide. All the previous experience in the world tells you nothing - because you are introducing something absolutely new.

And that leads to the next thing, which is, "Go for the touchdown pass." In football, if you are behind by six points and you have 30 seconds and you're on your own 20 (and that means you have to go 80 yards), and they've got everybody except the coach facing you on the line, what you do is you fall back. The quarterback falls back, he sends out the ends and everybody else as fast as they can, and he throws a 60-yard pass. If you catch it, you win; if it drops, you lose.

When you're in that situation, go for the touchdown pass. The only way to be a good copywriter is to get great results. To think of yourself as going for the breakthrough. And nobody can tell its power until the orders come in.

Always think statistically. You do not work with words. Think in terms of percentage points. That's what you should do.

Freshness Difference

Lorna Newman: Our controls run dry. A good control for us runs a year and a half to two years. We've never had a 17-year-old control. Why is that?

Schwartz: There are two things. Number one, your new format in selling in direct mail, the magalogs, is a very powerful format. Ergo, you are getting enormous numbers of people using the same format.

The more people that use your format, the more dangerous for you, because after a while, the person who gets your piece is having trouble distinguishing it from others'. And, of course, the mathematics are now known, and so even small companies realize that they can do it. That presents a constant challenge. Number two, I specialize in "ugly." I'm the lousiest layout man in the world. I do ugly layouts.

Why do I do ugly layouts? Because beauty looks much the same. It has a very narrow definition. Ugliness is randomness, which means that it's spread out. So there are a hundred different ways to be ugly and only two or three ways to be beautiful. So, the ugly thing in a world of beauty stands out.

Estee Lauder discovered that. Twenty years ago, when Revlon was just knocking them dead with this four-color printing and then everybody else came in, Helena Rubenstein, etc., Estee herself said, "Well, if we run four-color, we're gonna look like everybody else. Nobody's going to be able to tell us. How about sepia?" And she got a series of sepia ads that were stunningly beautiful but completely different. And when you open the magazines there, wham! There is Lauder.

So yes, the life of controls is probably shorter, and you are just going to have to innovate faster.

Think About Your "Does" Product

Question: Supposing we have a strong control that we think we have exhausted the market for. The message itself is strong. How much will a format change help?

Schwartz: You can get 20%-30% extra pull. That may not do it.

Let's think about it in a different way.

Take your product. Let's say it's got some pictures in it, and graphs.

Maybe just plain type. It's eight pages. That's your physical part.

That's all there is. Nobody in the world is going to buy that, though.

Nobody in the world cares about that.

Now let's push that physical product aside and let's get into the functional product. Functional product is what the physical product does for you. You've got a product there that does a certain number of things for you. Never think of what the product "is."A horse is an animal with four legs. It doesn't do anything for you. Think of what the product "does. "When you define something with a "does,î it becomes a functional definition instead of an academic definition; a dog that runs up and licks your face when you come home every night.

Your functional product - your "does" product - has immense number of "doeses." You have been tapping one specific strain of those "doeses."And that's been successful for you. But, you have pretty well exhausted that strain of "doeses." You have to go into the other "doeses." And that gives you an entire new mailing piece which may reach the same audience but from a different direction.

In my book, Breakthrough Copy, I give 27 different ways that you can "does" a product. Let's take one of them right now. If you are talking about money-making, why not bring in an audience? What does the product affect besides you? Who's going to look at you when you do this? We ran an ad for flowers 20 years ago that sold so many flowers we exhausted nurseries. And what it said, was, who ever head of 17,000 bloom from a single plant? We said,

"When you put this into the Earth, and you jump back (quickly), it explodes in flowers. And everybody in your neighborhood comes and they look. And people take home blooms because you've got so many you could never find a house big enough to put them in. And you've become the gardening expert for the entire neighborhood.

Multi-blossom plants had been selling fairly well before, but we brought the audience into copy as actors within it. So get another "does." There are all kinds of doeses. Just redo your product.

Is "Instant" Credible?

Stanton-Jones: Your company is called Instant Improvement. And all of the ads that I've read of yours promise improvement that is almost instantaneous. Also, in your Retirement Letter package that you are developing for us now you say, "Invest 45 minutes a month." But in our area, to demonstrate a result often takes months or even years.

Your copy says, "No, no. It is instantaneous." Do you think that this is credible?

Schwartz: I have a different view of your product this moment from this discussion, I think, than you did. I think what you hired me for was to give you a different view and infuriate you. Let's go back to my little Change piece. The Chang piece sells a book. Now you can't prove the book until you get the book. Ergo, there is no instant benefit.

Well, that's not true! I took an exercise from the book and I said this is the way you (the reader) proved the book. Practice it a second.

Remember, your selling piece is always part of your product; disconnected from the product and sent out advance of the product. It is the functional product that it includes, not the physical. In each issues of Retirement Letter you've been giving instant gratification.

You've been telling people that these are the three top bank stocks; there are the three top insurance stocks; this is the way to buy annuities; something XYZ annuity fund. That is instant gratification.

You have two powers in your present format. Number one, you have something that I call camouflage which means the first time a person picks up your magalog they think this is a magazine. That power being diluted at this time. The second is you this incredible power of demonstration. Demonstration is form of proof which takes place at the present moment. The person picks it up. He looks at it. I'm talking about your pieces now and he says, "Yes! I can prove this! You are giving instant gratification just as you have been giving instant gratification for years.

You have this incredible, strong, proven, product. It has all kinds of unique advantages nobody else has. It's been around for 20 years. It's never had a losing year. You've got 200,000 people who subscribe to it more than anyone else in the world. The man has an extremely powerful credential list. All that is there. But then, it's dealing with an incredibly sensitive subject: retirement. And the fear of being a failure at retirement. That's the worst fear any older person has. And what I tried to do and I'm not sure I could do it or I'm not sure you have accepted it, or I'm not sure it will pay off, is I try to make your benefits absolutely instantly accessible in ways that you have not made them before, by inventing a series of forms for you that the person simply sends in. And then I can give an extremely threatening headline and put an extremely great promise as its cure at the same time.

Almost anything that we do as publishers can be made instantaneous.

And people believe them. They are extremely powerful because nothing feels better than being proved right. And if you give them something that they can prove, they will really love it. That's what I'm trying to do. I think everything is instantaneous.

Bob King: When you think about it, there is only instant gratification in the present tense. No one goes to, say, medical school and says, "Gee, what I'm gonna work hard for ten years in school so I can be a doctor.

"Instead, you think about "Why do I do that today? Why am I doing that? "I do it because it feels right to me today to do that. If it didn't feel right, there's no way you'd work in the dark for ten years. So I think that you're constantly doing things that give you instant gratification. And really all the gratification really is in the present tense.

Schwartz: Very true, and very profound.

Think In Decimal Points

Copywriters should be completely conversant with statistics and returns. The worst thing you can do to your copywriters is to separate them from the returns of every list and every test and every cell.

Copywriters who write copy for the sake of copy and words alone are doomed to failure. If you keep your copywriters away from their results and their comparative results on every single test, they're not going to do very much for you.

Boardroom sends me thick packages of results. And I will spend three or four or five hours going over the results in detail for them. I think of myself as a person who creates 20% difference in returns. And I like decimal points. You've got to get those results. You can't know something from the outside. You have to know it inside.

1st Sale Must Build the 2nd Sale

Stanton-Jones: There's a piece of the puzzle that doesn't quite fit for me at the moment. And all the things that we do are trying to build toward the second sale. Does that violate this idea of instantaneous, miraculous change and improvement.

Schwartz: All mail order is dependent upon the second sale. Nobody really makes money on the first sale. You can, but it's an awfully strange way to run a company. If you get too much profit on your initial mailing, you immediately expand it to lists which are not doing quite as well, so that you can get more names and sales. When we sell books, we would very much love to have the people absolutely delighted with the book, because with the book comes a brochure advertising the next book! So our second sale is there. And we mail them every month. So our carrier is much like your carrier. Your newsletter is a carrier for further advertisements. That is so for us, too.

Why Infomercials Work

Think of television. In 1949, our agency bought time in that new medium called television, on ABC, on a half-hour program. We didn't know how to fill it so we wrote a program a day. How do you write a program a day? The only way you can write a program a day is to take the product and translate it into the program. There was a program called "The Answer Man, which was a regular program. People sent in questions; he answered them. So we decided, let's take the product - a piano course - and let's ask questions about the product for the entire 30 minutes, and then sell the product in the one-minute middle.

And so we said, "Ca my kid play? Can a five-year-old kid play? Can a five-year-old kid without arms play, etc.? "And we turned out one program a day! All talking about piano courses. Well, we didn't know it, but we invented the infomercial! Okay. We sold so darn many piano courses. And why did it work? Because we were demonstrating the product on the air.

Television infomercials really sell, but they also demonstrate.

Everybody should get a copy of the slicer commercial! The slicer is a demonstration. That is the product. And what is coming across the mail in your package is not the physical product, but the functional product. Demonstrations are sending the products to the person.

Selling to Current Subscribers

Newman: Our editors write special reports, and we sell them in inserts. It's not as spectacular copy. Mostly because we write it. Do you talk to subscribers differently from prospects, do you think?

Schwartz: I would test it. I would get the copywriter who wrote the promotion copy to write some of the subscriber follow-ups. Have them use the same copy. And see, whether it pulls more. If you have not tested it against another approach, perhaps y9ou're losing an opportunity.

Unknown: Every 'don't' is an opportunity. Just remember that. Now, it's an opportunity which is slippery. You may fall flat on your face because if you test another newsletter to the newsletter that you're selling, you may cut your renewals done. So you've got a two-stage test. Number one, what does this pull now? Number two, does it hurt renewals later on?

Are You Failing Enough?

Stanton-Jones: We recently had an experience where we used a well-known magazine copywriter with many soft-offer controls for magazines. He wrote us a package that did terribly. What's your advice? Do you think that that type of copywriter cannot work in our field? Do you think soft-offer copywriters can never work on hard-offer newsletters? Or is there a way to work with them differently?

Schwartz: I can give a few theories. Number one, maybe he just didn't have any rapport with your particular product at that time, and he missed. Number two, perhaps he's going for the jackpot. He tried harder; you took a bigger chance. It's very discouraging to work something that pulls within four or five percent of another offer. Then something's wrong. You're not taking enough of a chance. If you are running tests which are giving you small improvements, and if you are not running enough tests that are really flopping, then you are not doing your job.

Copywriters are crazy. And you want them crazy. They go for the big kill. And I would rather flop badly and succeed greatly than I would coming in with that little five percent boost. A very good copywriter is going to fail. If the guy doesn't fail, he's no good. He's got to fail. It hurts. But it's the only way to get the home runs the next time.

Postscript – What This Series Has To Do With You

Preamble

Before I launch into some very nice prose which is designed to entertain, educate, and enlighten you, I have to lay out some basics.

When you understand marketing and copywriting, *you can achieve, acquire, and accomplish anything you want – by helping everyone around you get what they want.* That's why this book was created – to help you do just that.

People are living a story that they are very serious about, for the most part. They think they have no choice in this matter.

What they don't know, mostly, is that story is being created by them and lasts as long as they want it to.

Your job as a marketer or copywriter, accept it or not, is to help them with their story by describing offers to them that they can use to push their story along.

The reason for this series of books is to bring you a collection of stories lived by some of the world's greatest copywriters and salepersons. When you study their stories, you'll then understand how marketing is actually done – not the way it's been sold as a subject since just before the Internet was invented.

Humankind hasn't changed much, if any, since we started writing down our histories. Our markets are the same as when they were bazaars in the local village square. What people want hasn't changed, their motivations haven't changed. Only our current circumstances.

We are each on a journey through the life we live out on this planet. High-tech or primitive, the basic human reactions are the same as they always have been, regardless of what we encounter on this journey.

The idea of a journey-story is what starts to tie up all the loose ends of marketing into a cohesive approach – an underlying system which explains all, resolves all. If you understand what motivates every person on Earth, then you can form your offer to help them along on that journey they are on. And they'll pay you well for this – which helps you on your own journey.

Life-journeys were defined years ago by a professor named Joseph Campbell. He wrote several books about how there is one common plot to all myths and legends. Campbell found that the stories which resonated through history, that were retold time and time again, were the ones which fit a certain pattern.

Campbell told of this story as a journey which every hero (or heroine) undertook. And this common journey-story can be as complicated or as simple as you'd like.

The very simplest is this:

Departing on the Journey

- The call to adventure, perhaps rejected at first
- Meeting a mentor or guide.
- Point of no Return, where the world transforms

Life-Changes

- A series of trials, temptations, and resolutions
- Atonement and rebirth – *total* paradigm shift
- Goal achievement

Returning

- Flight with the goal-solution
- Rescue by companions
- Recrossing back into normal life with new freedoms

The common players in every story:

- Hero or Heroine
- Helpers
- Goal or object being attained.

Marketers do their pitch to help a person along at one stage or another of their journey. Pitches all aren't all calls to adventure. You are offering products which symbolize something that is vital to that journey progress. Your pitch is another helper for whatever they are facing. It's up to you to know your potential customer or client to see what they need so you can fill it.

Breakthrough Copywriter - 78

As you study Campbell (recommended) and those who wrote about him (Vogler is a good study) you'll see this above description is pretty watered down. I've kept it simple so you can apply is in our "non-heroic" times.

It is the single story which is told over and over, regardless of circumstance. While there are as many variations as there are individuals on this planet, the basic plot is the same for everyone.

This is what I found to be the common thread through all Marketing and copywriting as well. If you go back to find the all-time great advertisements and marketing campaigns, you'll see that they tell a story.

- "Do You Make These Mistakes in English?"
- "They laughed when I sat down at the piano – but when I began to play..."
- "At 60 miles an hour the loudest noise in this new Rolls-Royce comes from the electric clock."

These are stories which sold over and over. Why? Because they help a person on their journey.

The products they buy are symbols which help them on their journey. Clothes tell the status of a person, they are the costume which helps that person get into or stay in character during the journey. Vehicles, electronic gadgets, houses – all these things make the journey easier or are tools which make that achievement possible.

You also have the reverse – where people are desperately working to avoid the journey in front of them, and seek continual distraction from what they know to be true.

The copywriter or marketer who knows these and a few other facts will be able to make sense of all the various "schools" and "brands" of marketing, as well as all the "guru-speak" which is out there.

What follows next are a few short essays which expand on this concept. I've left them as originally written – some of the points repeat what I've just told you. All I'm telling you here is simply a metaphor, a tool-set. Do with it what you will.

Test all this for yourself and throw away everything which doesn't work for you. Only then will you be able to use it effectively in your own marketing.

What Story are YOU Living?

People live in their own story. And that story controls their life.

People are pre-occupied with that story – how it will turn out, plot twists, happy or tragic ending, their story that runs their life. They listen to this story more than they listen to the people who are trying to talk to them in real life.

And, as the old phrase, they write their story as they go along, much as Shakespeare would write the play even as the actors rehearsed it.

People get their inspiration for that story from the other stories around them.

Their story is continually running in every person's head, constantly refined and improved by the stories they compare with it.

This comparing is what can get people into trouble. Or saves their bacon. It's truly a life or death scene from day to day. This explains the drama so many people go through, while others lead calm and cheerful lives. It's the story-line they follow.

People are in search of the perfect story. One that explains their life so far and gives them direction to follow.

The person who influences their story controls them - by their own choice. Any politician knows this. The really effective ones (like FDR, and similar) leave a feel-good "legacy" which takes decades to unravel the factual truth from the fictional story they wove. (The Great Depression was made worse and longer than it should have been.)

The bad politicians (Hitler, Mussolini, Stalin) weren't bad because of what they did (well, yes - but that's another story.) Let me rephrase that: They weren't bad *according to the people in their own country* – even for years after they were driven from power – because they consistently told a story which with their people wanted.

Hitler was going to return Germany to a level of prominence in the world that was unjustly taken away from them, back to global approval.

Some people in Russia even today long for a return to the "good old days" of Stalin and complete control over their lives – stable security.

People live a certain story in their life.

They compare the stories they hear and see with that internal story to see if they are living their life the right way - are they following the plot right, are they being the right character?

So when you tell a good story, you get elected. If you keep telling a good story (like FDR's "it was all the earlier guy's fault...") then people continue to like you and you stay in power. That's why U.S. Presidents are limited to two terms ever since.

Some people can tell a story too well for our own good.

Seriously. That's the way things are.

But let's back up.

I'm not counting on you believing me. In fact, I'm counting on you disbelieving me. Because until you start listening to the stories around you with a critical ear and eye, you will continue to live a life which takes all the money you make and leaves you nothing in return (except some expensive doo-dads, bumper stickers and yard signs.)

The old saying is true: out of 100 people graduating, 5 will retire wealthy, 10 will be able to retire at all, and the rest will be broke and dependent on the government or charity to keep them alive.

The difference is their story and who they let influence its outcome.

We aren't here to talk about politics. (It's just that they make such good punching bags, er... examples - when they are no longer around.)

The only difference between the people writing the ads which make you buy their stuff and the speech writers that make you vote for a certain young, good-looking politician is... Nothing.

They both use your emotions to get what THEY want.

Not what YOU want.

Yes, you have it all rationalized out that you did the right thing. But funny enough, when enough things break on that gorgeous chunk of metal in your driveway - you'll trade it in for another of the same brand.

The really good marketers find out what you want and offer it to you in a way that's natural for you to accept. The great copywriters hep you live your life the way you already think you want it.

People disagree on who the all-time legendary copywriters are. There are huge long lists of people you've never heard of, and how these people were Kings of their Heaps.

What I've done is to take all these lists and boil them down the the same few names which keep coming up.

Then I've studied *those* authors to see what they said worked for them - and found a few *other* authors to study.

Meanwhile, I took the same key datums all these authors said and boiled them down. (And decided to reproduce those I could as the simplest way of getting these books to you – in its own series.)

The final step was to boil even those down until when the steam cleared, there was just one nugget left in the bottom of that huge pot.

You've already been introduced to it:

Life is a journey-story.

The person can only figure out if their story is a good one if they compare it to other stories around them.

People who tell them stories which are similar to theirs can get them to do what they want.

This is called copywriting.

It is part of a subject called "marketing" - which is really just communication.

People who are known as "good talkers" or "good salespeople" or "great communicators" are all just marketing their own story in a way people want to hear it.

When you buy their stuff (or vote their way) you've decided that your story would be better if you took the action they told you to.

We are going to get to the main way these people get away with ordering you around.

But all these copywriters and speechwriters know one thing:

Your life-story is built from emotion.

In fact, all communication is built from emotion. Every word has some emotional connotation by itself, weak or strong. They draw their power from the words on either side. This is what gives poetry it's strength – and why Shakespeare is still so powerful, even though no one speaks that version of English these days.

Every good story involves you emotionally in the outcome. You sit in that theater, or in front of that TV, or in a "good" book - completely oblivious to everything around you - until it ends.

And then for days afterwards, you are still hearing that story go around in your thoughts.

If they told you a good enough story, you will hear it for years. You'll even change your life so that you are constantly reminded of their story by the various doo-dads you have around you.

It's not just buying the book or DVD or downloading that TED talk. (Or for some, playing that game over and over and over until you figure out how to win all the levels - or until the next version comes out...)

It's the story in it. Something in their story makes you want to have that outcome in your own story.

The emotions they used to tell their story is one you like to experience. So you keep coming back over and over.

Or you buy their products over and over. Or vote for that party over and over. Or watch that actor or actress over and over.

You have become one of the highest prizes. You're a client. Also known as a devoted fan.

But all is good. *All* stories are good ones.

Because you are just following your emotions. And you're always right.

That's the way you and I and everyone are wired.

Practically no one is immune. Well, statistically, it's between one in a million and one in ten billion. Those people are called "enlightened" and not much marketing works on them. (They already have everything they could ever need or want anyway - but that's another story.)

What you are probably wanting to know next is: how do I learn to write like this? Or - how do I learn to write my own story?

What's The Difference Between A Good And Bad Copywriter?

I was wandering around reading tons of material on writing sales pages, landing pages, scripts. I was studying headlines, subheadings, bullet points. I was absorbing the details of graphics and type-styles and colors.

I was trying to absorb all these details about the perfect marketing approach - and it was going nowhere. Just filling up my hard-drives and filling up my book-cases.

But I thought the next book or video or webinar would tell me the key point I was missing.

Bob Bly was the one to finally bust my balloon.

He said it was simple:

A good copywriter gets the sale.

Joe Sugarman said the same thing. So did most of the others when you look for it.

All these details about how to build the sales page were only valuable if they helped the ad do that one thing.

Some ad that is considered good copywriting helps the reader buy. More than just "wanting" to buy - they actually buy the stuff being talked about.

A good copywriter will make the person buy -- by pushing the right emotional buttons.

The whole point of copywriting is to get the person to act. To take out their credit card and buy whatever is being talked about.

A good copywriter tells the story that reader wants to hear.

Yes, we see a problem with this.

How do you keep someone like Hitler getting in charge again?

Practically, the only way you can do this is like the joke:

Q. *How do you get down from an elephant?*

A. *You don't. You get down from a goose.*

Get it? *Goose down.*

You change the world by changing your own story.

You can proof yourself up against those who only want you following their story. Then you can decide if it's somewhere you want to go.

Reading this and deciding for yourself if it works for you is the one way you can take charge over your own story.

I'll give you a lot of other books you can read, mostly about copywriting. The rest is up to you.

The next question is almost the same:

How do you start telling stories which will help people around you to live better lives?

And that is what the good copywriters are doing every day, with every ad or article.

They are telling people stories which enable them to take action and make their own life better in some way.

You see, good copywriting makes people feel better - and act.

Bad copywriting makes people feel worse - and act.

Poor copywriting doesn't get a person to act either way. And usually isn't read after the headline.

There are good emotions and bad emotions. Either type can get a person to act.

Constantly following bad emotions will wreck your life, however. This is why people who are constantly critical have few true friends.

Critical people look for stories which have a critical storyline in them. Because they need reasons to explain the actions they take.

People *decide* emotionally and *excuse* it logically.

Good copywriting will give the logical explanation for buying. These are known as "features." But the person decides to buy based on the "benefits" which are always emotional.

Perry Marshall is known for a phrase, "Nobody who bought a drill actually wanted a drill, they wanted a hole."

(He isn't the first one to notice it, but he's the one known for saying it.)

"Wanting" is emotional. And there is some sort of emotion behind and before that "want."

You want a hole because

- people will look up to you,
- you'll have better control in your life,
- it will make you a more secure future,
- you'll finally be part of an exclusive group,
- etc.
- etc.

Meanwhile, you buy that expensive drill you are going to use once or twice and store in your shop for years later. Like most power tools owned by consumers. (Professionals are different - they'll own several. Some are called "backups.")

As you read down the sales page, you'll go through all the emotional reasons for buying, and then they'll tell you the logical reasons why you're right.

Right down to the P.S. - which tells you again to buy that item right now.

Valuable Copywriters Are Different.

Valuable copywriters are there to improve their own lives by improving the lives of people they talk to.

They are not good copywriters or bad copywriters - they are not poor, if they are valuable to others.

People will follow you to the end of the earth if you are consistently handing out valuable stuff.

While value is just a matter of perception, there is an underlying principle older than written history which haunts copywriters who try to short-cut this process:

You can't get without giving. You'll only *get* according to what you *give*.

This is known as the "Golden Rule" - among other things.

Zig Ziglar said it this way, *"You will get all you want in life if you help enough other people get what they want."*

Look this over carefully.

People run their lives by emotion. So a person who is able to influence their emotions can take over running all these lives. Or so some people think.

Actually, you can only get and keep a following if you are always giving valuable stuff out.

Yes, they'll pay you ungodly sums for this stuff.

But only if it's valuable - and continues to be so.

Even if you talk to other people's emotions - you'll only get what you give out. To the degree you honestly help others is the degree you'll get the help you need.

Right about now is the point where you realize I'm ruining everything.

Because from here on out, you are going to see through all the sales pages you read, all the commercials you hear or watch, every story you pick up.

You're going to look to see whether that person is giving something that's actually valuable. To you.

You're going to pull back the curtains and watch that "Wizard of Oz" do their stuff.

Doesn't mean you aren't going to buy. But it does mean what you will be in better control over what you buy and the actual "why" you are buying.

Doesn't mean you aren't emotionally involved.

But it does mean that you are going to start writing your own story.

How do you tell what's a "good" story?

Again, you're looking for the "goose down."

Work it backwards:

- You're trying to succeed every day you live.
- The storyline you are following has certain goals to be successful.
- Some activities and people you meet won't help you make your goals.
- You'll attract what you need to achieve those goals (or get what you want) by helping others achieve similar goals.

How A Story "Works"

There are many, many forms of stories. They are called by many names - "meme", legend, icon, quest, journey...

A story works because of the emotion it contains and how its presented.

This is the sole reason for the success of bestseller books, movies, songs, brands.

Sole reason.

Stories are alive to the degree they allow people to participate in the emotion they hold. Stories grow as people spread them.

Stories are tuned, like any music or instrument, to reach a certain audience, wide or narrow.

They become a "classic" when they are tuned so that generations later they are still being told – even though the language and even their model has changed.

Shakespeare's "Romeo and Juliet" became West Side Story. The Gospel of Jesus has continued to reach wide audiences in all the various ways it's been told – more recently, "The Robe," "The Greatest Story Ever Told," and "The Passion of the Christ" are several notable recent ones. Wikipedia lists 29 English ones, and five other languages.

Christopher Vogler wrote one of the best guidebooks to understanding Joseph Campbell's works. Called "The Writer's Journey," it tells how successful films were created (the "Star Wars" series for one) based on that singular "monomyth" plot.

In the introduction to the Third Edition, he also points out that a "tuned" story will actually create a physical response in the body:

I learned... to listen to my body as a judge of a story's effectiveness. I realized that the good stories were affecting the organs of my body in various ways, and the really good ones were stimulating more than one organ. An effective story grabs your gut, tightens your throat, makes your heart race and your lungs pump, brings tears to your eyes or an explosion of laughter to your lips. If I wasn't getting some kind of physiological reaction from a story, I knew it was only affecting me on an intellectual level and therefore it would probably leave audiences cold.

Vogler then went on to write an entire chapter on that very subject at the end of that edition.

Stories are that powerful.

Marketing stories which were well-crafted have won awards even through they sold no product. The industry award for advertising, the Clio, used to have this "curse" attached to it – agencies which had won the award were usually not in business by the following year.

You have to tell your marketing story in the way which gets <u>action</u>.

Bottom line.

Emotions are used to forward that goal. People "think" with their emotions, true. But no ad is worth anything to anyone unless it achieves and improves sales.

Wherever you are influencing people to continue with their journey-story, you have to end up actually getting them to do something.

This is when the story "works."

When Is a (Marketing) Story "Sensible?"

When it balances logic and emotion.

Let's jump way out there: There is no time, there is only Now. (This is the core secret hidden in plain site in all philosophies, if you dig far enough.) And we keep track of incidents that make up our "time-track" in order to make sense of what we are doing Now.

This is why any two people don't see the same accident in front of them. They both are recording and accepting the recording which balances both their logic and their emotion.

This is why history is constantly being re-written – by historians and individuals.

History is never pat, set, or definite. Like the old saying, "the only thing constant is change."

What "makes sense" is when you have that balance of logic and emotion.

Emotion is created. It literally means "move out." It isn't perception, it's your own patterned response to what you see or hear, or taste, etc.

Feelings are a closer description of what you perceive. Of course, that's booby-trapped by our language as well.

Mostly, you can only feel stuff that happens to you. You can feel peace. You can feel happy. You can feel good. Most feelings, if not all, are nouns, not verbs.

The one exception that comes to mind is "love". You can feel love, and you can love someone else.

But there's a trick to that word. It's not a feeling or emotion. It *creates* feelings and emotions. Love is creation. This again is one of these oldest traditions from pre-history beliefs.

Love even created hate.

Hate is only an emotion. It's out-facing. You can hold onto hate, even "hate" yourself – but the meaning just means "trying to destroy."

But in this universe, nothing is truly destroyed. Only Love can dissolve things back to their original elements.

Look back on your own life and you should be able to find enough examples of this to prove it to yourself.

Hate and negative emotions only work to physically re-arrange the shape of things around you. They'll make someone sick instead of healing them. They'll wreck relationships instead of building them.

Negative emotions are never sensible. Because they're too emotional.

Before we go too far down this line, let me point out that feelings are also created – by Love.

Love makes sense more times than not. Of course you can have a head-over-heels "true love" which won't logically make much sense. However, the people who work to make sense out of this will create a new world where their attraction to each other does make sense – and the new world they create (as long as they continue to create it) will be in perfect harmony and give them all the success they want.

- - - -

In sales copywriting, you have to achieve this balance.

People will decide emotionally and justify logically.

Your sales copy has to enable the reader to become the hero of the piece.

Hero's make sense out of nonsensical situations.

They triumph over evil to create a new reality.

Study Joseph Campbell's various books ("Hero With a Thousand Faces", "The Power of Myth") and you'll see that all the myths, legends, psychologies, and stories through the ages really boil down to a single plot (sequence).

It's this plot which also runs through all copywriting. Well, all *good* copywriting.

Bad copywriting doesn't tell a complete story or get even close.

You get involved with some simple ad and then they pitch something which is unrelated.

They are talking about a hero surviving a war, and then try to have you buy a refrigerator.

Because those copywriters don't understand what they are doing. They think they do. And they get some sales to prove it. But what they are doing is only repeating something they saw somewhere else and changing it.

Not improving it – changing it.

They don't understand how to make something make sense.

Heroes decide and act emotionally. But think logically. It will always be a surprise.

Logic isn't surprising, usually. Emotions aren't surprising. But the solution which is sensible can be very surprising.

This is your (the reader's) "Ah-ha!" moment.

And that is where the sale is made.

Because that is where they decide to act.

When it makes perfect sense.

Versions of AIDA - the Song Sung Forever.

AIDA means Attract, Interest, Desire, Action.

There are as many versions of this as there are fish in the ocean.

They all sing the same song with different verses. But the hero always wins.

When you take apart the conventional sales page, it's just the Hero's Journey again:

> *Call to Adventure – Threshold – Transformation – Return*

> - or -

1. Adventure Invitation (Headline)
2. Threshold is passed (Subheading, emotional benefits, "USP")
3. Hero is transformed (logical reasons, features, objections answered)
4. Hero Returns with a Gift (PS, buys.)

Bob Bly had it this way:

The successful ad:

1. Gains attention
2. Focuses on the customer
3. Stresses benefits
4. Differentiates you from the competition
5. Proves its case
6. Establishes credibility
7. Builds value
8. Closes with a call to action

Victor Schwab wrote this over 70 years ago:

1. Get Attention

2. Show People An Advantage

3. Prove It

4. Persuade People To Grasp This Advantage

5. Ask For Action

These are all the same, really.

Just telling a story people want to hear.

And the success of that sales story is how well the copywriter tells it.

You need to know *why* as well as *how* to write good copy.

That's what this book is here for.

A good engineer bases his designs on proved principles, but listens to his intuition, too. The Wright Brothers combining their bicycle weight-lightening principles with aerodynamics they learned as children sledding – were able to get their machines off the ground with the inefficient motors of that day.

Copywriters won't just copy other's work, but will understand why these worked and then convert that success to their own product-push.

For me, once I was finally persuaded that I needed to learn this material to really make my sales take off, I then found myself surrounded by wannabe's – who were simply parroting people who had done the in-depth training in this subject.

I learned early to follow those people who had tested what actually produced sales and then slightly varied the text to see if this could be tweaked.

From this we got *"Do You Make These Mistakes in English?"* which ran for 40 years. And *"They laughed when I sat down at the piano – but when I began to play…"* which ran for 20 years. Also, this modern one: *"At 60 miles an hour the loudest noise in this new Rolls-Royce comes from the electric clock."*

Proved headlines, copy, pitches. That's what you should be studying. Not just having huge "swipe files" you can copy and use. Because they won't do you any good until you actually know how they work.

AIDA is a song which was known to the bazaar merchants in times before history. The successful ones anyway.

To learn to sing this song effectively, you need to study those who studied why.

Are You Really Real?

The worst failures and best successes I've seen were those where the story matched up - or didn't – with the writer-teller.

You can read these Internet Marketing pitches and wonder how they made all this money they claimed. Because they're selling junk – over and over and over.

Sure, most of them don't really make it big.

But I was studying someone who had actually made himself a huge hit in his industry. Yet he really didn't know what he was doing. Made millions. Almost accidentally.

His real story was more interesting than the one he pitched.

Because it was real.

Yes, there are flukes out there. People who get rich when there was no reason they did – or the rules were changed later so no one could really follow their model and make the same success.

So his name isn't one of the ones to study.

He's the realest fake I've seen. And almost lost the millions he'd made.

And when you tear apart his sales pitches to find out why they're successful – you'll see that they follow "the pattern", but have gaping holes in them.

They aren't stories you could follow. Because he told his own rag-to-riches story of bringing one book to a bunch of marketers where the whole industry didn't have a clue. And people followed him, bought his book, because it was definite and preached success.

He was determined to succeed. He persisted. After a dozen years, he became an "overnight" success. The idea he pitched was that he had become a millionaire in a little over 1 ½ years.

But he didn't. It took him a couple of decades of persistently learning from failures.

When you tear apart his book, it's filled with partial truths – not those which would make anyone but him actually rich.

Because he wasn't really interested in making others rich, just himself.

When you see someone who is arrogant, and preaches arrogance as a success route, you know he's ready to fail and take you with him. Because arrogance won't make any long-term success.

Success is built on making everyone around you successful. Ray Kroc (McDonald's) and Sam Walton (Wal-Mart) made more people into millionaires than they could count.

They aren't the only ones. You can just see their backstory easier.

Being the best of the best – and not letting anyone else shine as bright as you – is the sure route to failure.

When you can take a person apart and see the brilliant facade built on fakery – that's when you know that everyone that person mentions is just another fake.

You'll also see that those referenced guys are also fakes.

Blind leading the blind. And you can't trust anything they say.

What you'll see written here is from the people who honestly want to help you succeed.

"Accidental Millionaires who lose it all" is not what we want to study. "Millionaires who make millionaires" is.

Real is being useful. Real is making sense.

Building a backstory from deceit won't make a solid foundation for any business.

Really real is being transparent down to your core and giving away far more value than you actually sell in goods.

The Golden Rule works all the time, all day (and night) long. How you treat others is how you'll be treated. Keep looking down on people from "on-high" based on a false route no one else can follow - and you'll eventually and rightfully be shown up as a fake.

Money made by selling drugs which ruin people's lives won't stay with you. Any criminal is ultimately brought to justice – by their own hands.

Here's the secret that made this one person rich:

In any area, you can sell more training than you can anything else.

Because most people won't carry through on your lessons – and will be buying book after book, course after course, webinar after webinar.

That's where the real money is. That's what made this guy rich.

When you read this guy's book, you see him tell this right in the pages and his videos about it.

But he's not the only one. There are several fakes in the industry he came from.

The reason: the industry (multi-level-marketing) depends to a great deal on "fake it to make it." To succeed in any MLM, you nearly have to join a cult. (There are some few which are decent and don't depend on this.)

Up to this point, it's meant a personal belief system which you "infect" others to believe in as much as you. And then get them to infect others the same way. Starting with friends and family.

Nothing has the failure rate that MLM has as a single industry. Because the few who can really motivate masses to follow their lead are just one in a million.

Network Marketing is built on the backs of people who want to start a home business, but don't have a clue. (Not that it can't be done, but this industry is led by the blind.)

The Internet has both been the blessing and downfall of these schemes. Because MLM can now reach people easier than ever, they now have a faster turnover and higher failure rate than ever before.

It's taken this deep study of copywriting to separate out these facts from the fluff.

There are a *huge* number of people out there who are wannabe's. They make their living putting on a show, because they know the bulk of the people out there won't spend the time they need to invest to really learn and apply this or any subject. Such marketers are the ones who popularize the "get rich quick concept," *even though they know it's false.* They also tell you marketing is just a numbers racket – and build spam empires from short-cuts.

Breakthrough Copywriter - 100

Those who win in copywriting study the leaders who have done the testing and found what really works, every time.

Those who are the effective trainers have built courses based on people who have done the testing to prove what works – hundreds, if not thousands of cases.

Follow the really real, the ones that make sense.

Follow the ones who have tested and know.

Why These Stories Are Here

You can only be yourself.

Because you decided to be an individual a long time ago.

It's when you decided to be "good" and then to be the "best" that your life started really taking off.

That's the only type of story you can really tell.

And the stories you tell based on your own beliefs will the be most effective stories you can write.

By writing, you'll find what beliefs you have. The stuff you can't get to "turn out right" will be stuff that isn't you. It's not based on your own beliefs. It's trying to be someone you aren't.

How you learn to write stories is to spend the needed years learning the subject. There are no real shortcuts.

But all the writing you've done up to this point counts.

You're finally going to have to learn from people who have studied others people, and who have done testing to prove the basic principles behind every success out there.

These people were found by seeing who the popular copywriters were, finding who they referenced, and then finding who *those* people studied. The first two layers of that onion generally could be discarded.

It just didn't matter about popularity.

Results mattered.

The below authors routinely got results. And people who studied them got results.

Some are fairly unknown today, not their fault. However, if you boil down all the books here, you'd see how the ones which are now almost unknown could be revived...

- **How to Win Friends and Influence People** – Dale Carnegie is known by the Guinness Book of World Records for critiquing more speeches than any person in known history. He found that people wanted to know these two subjects. His book is based on the study of

solutions people found. It evolved from a pamphlet to a correspondence course to another all-time bestselling book.
- **Scientific Advertising** and **My Life in Advertising**– Claude Hopkins was the first to test the effectiveness of his ads by actual sales. He was the first to use coupons to do "split-testing" on two or more different versions of copy.
- **The Untold Story Behind Advertising** – Albert D. Lasker ran the most successful advertising office on the planet for over 40 years. He hired Claude Hopkins and paid him more than ever before for a copywriting job. This book tells how Advertising came of age and the changes it went through.
- **Tested Sentences That Sell** – Elmer Wheeler was a testing pioneer – having tested 105,000 selling statements for 5,000 products. He invented the phrase, "Sell the Sizzle, not the Steak" and summed up his philosophy as *"Don't think so much about what you want to say as about what the prospect wants to hear– then the response you will get will more often be the one you are aiming for."*
- **How to Write a Good Ad** – Victor Schwab was known for his testing with coded coupons. This book gives examples of 100 all-time winning headlines and tells why they work.
- **Robert Collier Copywriting Course** – Robert Collier was known as a highly successful copywriter long before his success in Self-Help books. He still ranks to day as one of the premier copywriters. This excerpts the key chapters from his famous "Letter Book."
- **The What, How and Why of Advertising** – John E. Kennedy revolutionized marketing when he first defined advertising as *Salesmanship in Print*. This is his two collected works, "Reason Why Advertising" and "Intensive Advertising."
- **Eugene Schwartz' Breakthrough Advertising** – this long out of print classic was unable to be reproduced. However, I tell you where you can download your copy to study and learn from a true master. It even surprised the author to learn that his simple book was

making non-marketers into millionaires by thoroughly understanding how markets work and how to get your product known in them.

Some extras:

- **How to Write Ad Copy That Works** – J. George Frederick compiled 22 of the then World's Greatest Advertising Writers of that time into a single book review. A great side-check on what you've learned.
- **How to Get Sales Without Having to "Sell"** - Works by Orison Swett Marden and Edward Berman point out how modern online sales work (even before the Internet) – where the buyer is in charge of the sales cycle. In order to understand advertising, I found these books to explain the basics of true salesmanship: empathy and care for the customer.
- **Breezy** – by J. George Frederick. The amusing story of a young lad who applies the simple basics of advertising to his sales, quickly rising up the ranks in his company applying what he knew.
- **Obvious Adams** – by Robert R. Updegraff. The story of a person who simply observed the products around him and then patterned his marketing on common sense.

Once you have all the above down, you can then compare what has worked for centuries to what the modern marketers are saying works.

And then your story will have wings.

How to Use this Book to Get Everything You Could Possibly Want

There is a simple reason this postscript is at the back of every book in this series:

You need to study all these books to become the best marketer you can.

Because, even mediocre and mis-trained copywriters writing for cheesy products can become millionaires with a few hackneyed, trite "formulas."

The reason I undertook this study was that one example I used earlier – the marketer who was more fake than real. All he really did was to succumb to the easy money being made in Internet Marketing, when you have these "guru's" who have amassed huge lists selling essentially junk to people who would buy it on hope. Then they would cross-sell each other's products to their lists and the cycle would continue with any new product any of them came out with.

Problem was – they weren't actually helping anyone really improve their life.

Here's the proven breakdown of what happens with a training product "guaranteed to make you a millionaire from your own home business" -

- Only 3% of the people who buy the product will actually finish the course.
- 3% of *those* will actually apply what they learned to break even.
- 3% of *those* will become an outrageous success – usually due to having already been trained by several previous training courses they took, not just this one.

The result – 1 in 1,000 will make their money back. 1 in 10,000 will become an flaming success and wind up as an example on info-mercials. (With 9,999 chances for refunds.)

But you are different.

In just this short postscript, I've told you everything you need to know in order to make very successful copywriting. The motivations and explanations for why humankind think and act as they do isn't found in any other book. (Well, just the one I wrote on "Get Your Self Scam Free.")

Because I wrote that book after I'd gotten scammed and wanted to find out why so it never happened again.

Scammers use the same techniques as honest marketers. It's just how they go about it.

An old adage about advertising says that great advertising with a poor product will run that company out of business. Mediocre advertising with a great product will make incredible amounts of money.

You can have everything you ever wanted if you

- Have a great product,
- Market it honestly,
- Write your copy brilliantly.

The copywriter's job is to get that product repaired if it's flawed.

Otherwise, you are going to have to fAdvertising Review Notesind another client – that company isn't going to be around for very long once people find out that the product sucks.

Know what you want out of your own journey-story before you start down that path with any old company willing to hire you.

Get an honest company with a great product and then promote it to the heavens – then watch whatever you really want in life show up.

Too simple. It's the reason that "Honesty is the Best Policy" is still retold today.

You have a right to everything you earn.

Do good – and earn everything you could want.

Resources

Get the rest of the Masters of Marketing Series:

- **Breakthrough Copywriter – A Field Guide to Eugene M. Schwartz Advertising Genius** by Dr. Robert C. Worstell
- **How to Write a Good Ad** by Victor O. Schwab
- **My Life in Advertising** by Claude C. Hopkins
- **Obvious Adams: The Story of a Successful Marketer** by Robert R. Updegraff
- **The Robert Collier Copywriting Course** by Robert Collier
- **Scientific Advertising** by Claude C. Hopkins
- **Tested Sentences That Sell** by Elmer Wheeler
- **The Untold Story of Advertising** based on lectures by Albert D. Lasker
- **The What, How, and Why of Advertising by** – John E. Kennedy
- **How to Sell Without "Selling"** by Orison Swett Marden and Edward Berman
- **How to Write Ad Copy that Works** by Justus George Fredericks

Available from most online book distributors and in print.

Visit Midwest Journal Press for more materials and related books

http://mastersofmarketingsecrets.midwestjournalpress.com/

Bonus

Get Related Materials
from Our Business Guide Library

Instant Access - Join Here

Click or type into your browser:

http://livesensical.com/go/byob/

CPSIA information can be obtained
at www.ICGtesting.com
Printed in the USA
LVHW111230061218
599462LV00001B/125/P